Editor
Eric Migliaccio

Editor In Chief
Ina Massler Levin, M.A.

Illustrator
Clint McKnight

Cover Artist
Brenda DiAntonis

Art Production Manager
Kevin Barnes

Art Coordinator
Renée Christine Yates

Imaging
James Edward Grace
Nathan P. Rivera
Craig Gunnell

Publisher
Mary D. Smith, M.S. Ed.

NONFICTION READING COMPREHENSION
Grade 6 — Science
Ideal for Test Practice
Includes Standards & Benchmarks

Author
Ruth Foster, M.Ed.

The classroom teacher may reproduce the materials in this book and/or CD for use in a single classroom only. The reproduction of any part of this book and/or CD for other classrooms or for an entire school or school system is strictly prohibited. No part of this publication may be transmitted or recorded in any form without written permission from the publisher with the exception of electronic material, which may be stored on the purchaser's computer only.

Teacher Created Resources, Inc.
12621 Western Avenue
Garden Grove, CA 92841
www.teachercreated.com
ISBN: 978-1-4206-8037-9

©2008 Teacher Created Resources, Inc.
Reprinted, 2016
Made in U.S.A.

Teacher Created Resources

Table of Contents

Introduction 3
Using This Book 4
The Stories—New Words—The Writing Link—The Questions—The Test Link—The Thrill of Science
Meeting Standards 8
Science Stories

What Swallowed Camels 9	The Mammal with a Suit of Armor 75
Why Mari Said, "No!" 12	Moon Rocks 78
The Amazing Jumper 15	Injecting Poison on Purpose 81
Conjoined Twins 18	The 5,000-Year-Old Man 84
Identical Trees 21	A Quiver of Cobras 87
The Extreme Sport of Paper-Folding 24	The Price of a Crooked Finger 90
What Was Not a Grave 27	May I Draw a Round Perimeter? 93
A Town That Gets No Sun 30	Why Warm Flowers? 96
45,000 Years of Penguin Droppings 33	Space Animals 99
Finding the Counterfeit Coin 36	"Operation Successful, Patient Died" 102
Amphibian Escort 39	The Missing Crust 105
Blisters—To Pop or Not 42	The Abandoned City of the Future 108
The World's First Life Preserver 45	Ant Farmers 111
What Is It? 48	The Human Ecosystem 114
Getting Stung on Purpose 51	The Richter Scale 117
A Season for Potholes 54	What the Meteorologists Found 120
The True Story Behind DNA 57	Observing the Jackal 123
Strange Stomach Stories 60	Disease Detectives 126
A Parachute and a Shark 63	The Astronomer with the Metal Nose 129
A True Case from 1856 66	Taking a Volcano's Pulse 132
What Came First 69	The King of Soaring 135
The Most Expensive Rattle 72	Tuberculosis and a Cave 138

Answer Sheets 141
Bibliography 142
Answer Key 144

Introduction

* **Science is thrilling.**
  Think of discovering a 5,000-year-old mummy in a glacier.

* **It has changed our world.**
  Think of how an entire city had to be abandoned and all of its residents evacuated forever because of a nuclear disaster.

* **It affects our lives daily.**
  Think of how thanks to the work of Joseph Lister, doctors must now clean their hands and instruments between surgeries and patients.

Reading comprehension can be practiced and improved while coupled with science instruction. This book presents short, fascinating science stories. The stories were chosen to arouse curiosity; augment basic science facts and concepts taught at the sixth-grade level; and introduce a world of ideas, people, and animals.

A page of questions follows each story. These questions will provide students familiarity with different types of test questions. In addition, the practice they provide will help students develop good testing skills. Questions are written so that they lead students to focus on what was read. They provide practice for finding the main idea, as well as specific details. They provide practice in deciphering new and unknown vocabulary words. In addition, the questions encourage students to think beyond the facts. For example, every question set has an analogy question in which students are expected to think about the relationship between two things and find a pair of words with the same type of relationship. Other questions provide an opportunity for students to extrapolate and consider possible consequences relevant to the information provided in the story.

The book is designed so that writing can be incorporated into every lesson. The level of writing will depend on what the teacher desires, as well as the needs of the students.

Lessons in *Nonfiction Reading Comprehension: Science, Grade 6* meet and are correlated to the Mid-continent Research for Education and Learning (McREL) standards. They are listed on page 8.

A place for *Nonfiction Reading Comprehension: Science, Grade 6* can be found in every classroom or home. It can be a part of daily instruction in time designated for both reading and science. It can be used for both group and individual instruction. Stories can be read with someone or on one's own. *Nonfiction Reading Comprehension: Science, Grade 6* can help students improve in multiple areas, including reading, science, critical thinking, writing, and test-taking.

Using This Book

The Stories

Each story in *Nonfiction Reading Comprehension: Science, Grade 6* is a separate unit. For this reason, the stories can (but do not have to be) read in order. A teacher can choose any story that coincides with classroom activity.

Stories can be assigned to be read during science or reading periods. They can be used as classroom work or as supplemental material.

Each story is five paragraphs long. The stories range from 325–350 words in length. They are written at the sixth-grade level and have the appropriate sentence structure.

New Words

Each story includes a list of eight new words. Each of the new words is used a minimum of two times in the story. New words may sometimes have an addition of a simple word ending such as "s," "ed," or "ing." The new words are introduced in the story in the same order that they are presented in the new word list. Many of the new words are found in more than one story. Mastery of the new words may not come immediately, but practice articulating, seeing, and writing the words will build a foundation for future learning.

* A teacher may choose to have the students read and repeat the words together as a class.

* While it is true that the majority of the words are defined explicitly or in context in the stories, a teacher may choose to discuss and define the new words before the students begin reading. This will only reinforce sight-word identification and reading vocabulary.

* A teacher may engage the class in an activity in which students use the new word in a sentence. Or, the teacher may use the word in two sentences. Only one sentence will use the word correctly. Students will be asked to identify which sentence is correct. For example, one new word is *gaping*. The teacher might say,

    "The students, their mouths gaping open in surprise, stared in shock at the gorilla that had just entered the classroom."

    "The students, their mouths gaping tightly shut, stared in shock at the gorilla that had just entered the classroom."

* A teacher may also allow students to choose one new word to add to their weekly spelling list. This provides students with an opportunity to feel part of a decision-making process, as well as gain "ownership" over new words. In addition, practice spelling sight words reinforces the idea that we can learn to recognize new words across stories because there is consistency in spelling.

* A teacher may choose to have students go through the story after it is read and circle each new word one or two times.

Using This Book (cont.)

The Writing Link

A teacher may choose to link writing exercises to the science stories presented in the book. All writing links reinforce handwriting and spelling skills. Writing links with optional sentence tasks reinforce sentence construction and punctuation.

* A teacher may choose to have a student pick one new word from the list of new words and write it out. Space for the word write-out is provided in this book. This option may seem simple, but it provides students with opportunities to take control. The students are not overwhelmed by the task of the word write-outs because they are choosing the word. It also reinforces sight-word identification. If a teacher has begun to instruct students in cursive writing, the teacher can ask them to write out the word twice, once in print and once in cursive.

* A teacher may choose to have the students write out a complete sentence using one of the new words. The sentences can by formulated together as a class or as individual work. Depending on other classroom work, the teacher may want to remind students about capital letters and ending punctuation.

* A teacher may require the students to write out a sentence after the story questions have been answered. The sentence may or may not contain a new word. The sentence may have one of the following starts:

    - I learned . . .
    - I thought . . .
    - Did you know . . .
    - An interesting thing about . . .

If the teacher decides on this type of sentence formation, the teacher may want to show students how they can use words directly from the story to help form their sentences, as well as make sure that words in their sentences are not misspelled. For example, for the first paragraph in the selection titled "What Swallowed Camels" (page 10), possible sample sentence write-outs may be as follows:

"I learned that one day the Horn of Africa may become a new continent."

"I thought it was interesting that the Earth's crust is made up of 15 moveable plates of rock."

"Did you know that some plates are drifting apart, while others are drifting closer?"

"An interesting thing about Ethiopia's gaping hole is that it has grown to one-third of a mile (.5 k) long."

This type of exercise reinforces spelling and sentence structure. It also teaches responsibility: students learn to go back to the story to check word spelling. It also provides elementary report-writing skills. Students are taking information in a story source and reporting it in their own sentence construction.

Using This Book (cont.)

The Questions

Five questions follow every story. Questions always contain one main-idea, one specific-detail, and one analogy question.

* The main-idea question pushes students to focus on the topic of what was read. It allows practice in discerning between answers that are too broad or too narrow.

* The specific-detail question requires students to retrieve or recall a particular fact mentioned in the story. Students gain practice referring back to a source. They also are pushed to think about the structure of the story. Where would this fact most likely be mentioned in the story? Which paragraph would most likely contain the fact to be retrieved?

* The analogy question pushes students to develop reasoning skills. It pairs two words mentioned in the story and asks students to think about how the words relate to each other. Students are then asked to find an analogous pair. Students are expected to recognize and use analogies in all course readings, written work, and in listening. This particular type of question is found on many cognitive-functioning tests.

* The remaining two questions are a mixture of vocabulary, identifying what is true or not true, inference, and extrapolation questions. Going back and reading the word in context can always answer vocabulary questions. The inference questions are often the most difficult for many students, but they provide practice for what students will find on standardized tests. They also encourage students to think beyond the story and to think critically about how facts can be interpreted or why something works.

The Test Link

Standardized tests have become obligatory in schools throughout our nation and around the world. There are certain test-taking skills and strategies that can be developed by using this resource.

* Students can answer the questions on the page by filling in the circle of the correct answer, or you may choose to have your students use the answer sheet located at the back of the book (page 141). Filling in the bubble page provides students with practice responding in a standardized-test format.

* Questions are presented in a mixed-up order, though the main idea question is always placed in the numbers one, two, or three slots. The analogy question is always placed in the three, four, or five slots. This mixed-up order provides practice with standardized-test formats, where reading-comprehension passages often have main-idea questions, but these type of questions are not necessarily placed first.

Using This Book (cont.)

The Test Link (cont.)

* A teacher may point out to students that often a main-idea question can be used to help focus on what the story is about. A teacher may also point out that an analogy question can be done any time, since it is not crucial to the main focus of the story.

* A teacher may want to remind students to read every answer choice. Many students are afraid of not remembering information. Reinforcing this tip helps them to remember that on multiple-choice tests, one is identifying the best answer, not making up an answer.

* A teacher may choose to discuss the strategy of eliminating wrong answer choices to find the correct one. Teachers should instruct students that even if they can only eliminate one answer choice, their guess would have a better chance of being right. A teacher may want to go through several questions to demonstrate this strategy. For example, in the "What Swallowed Camels" selection, there is the following question:

> **5.** From the story, one can tell that in one's lifetime
> (a) one will see a new continent.
> (b) one will notice the continents drifting.
> (c) one will not notice the continents drifting.
> (d) one will see the Arabian plate become a new continent.

A student may not be able to spot the answer immediately, as it is never specifically stated that one cannot see the continents drifting. A student may, though, be able to eliminate wrong answer choices. For example, a student may realize after reading all the answer choices, that if "a" or "d" is correct, one will have noticed the continents drifting. Therefore, if "a" or "d" is correct, then so too must be "b." As there cannot be two correct answers, neither "a" nor "d" can be correct. Guessing at this point gives a child a 50% chance at choosing the correct answer.

Having now to check only two answer choices, the student can refer back to the story where the amount of drifting is mentioned (paragraph 3) or how long it might take for a new continent to appear (paragraph 5). Paragraph 3 states the drifting is very small, and paragraph states that if a new continent appears, it will be in one million years. Either paragraph leads a child to answer choice "c."

The Thrill of Science

The challenge of writing this book was to allow students access to the thrills of science while understanding that many science words or concepts are beyond the sixth-grade reading level. It is hoped that the range of stories and the ways concepts are presented reinforces basic science concepts, all while improving basic reading-comprehension skills. It is also hoped that the students' imaginations are whetted. After reading each story, students will want to question and explore the subject.

Meeting Standards

Listed below are the McREL standards for Language Arts Level 2 (Grades 3–5).

> Copyright 2004 McREL
> Mid-Continent Research for Education and Learning
> 2250 S. Parker Rd, Suite 500
> Aurora, CO 80014
> Telephone: 303-337-0990
> Website: www.mcrel.org/standards-benchmarks

McRel Standards are in **bold**. Benchmarks are in regular print. All lessons meet the following standards and benchmarks unless noted.

Uses the general skills and strategies of the writing process

- Uses a variety of strategies to edit and publish written work (*All lessons where writing or typing a complete sentence option is followed.*)

Uses the stylistic and rhetorical aspects of writing

- Uses a variety of sentence structures to expand and embed ideas (*All lessons where writing or typing a complete sentence option is followed.*)

Uses grammatical and mechanical conventions in written compositions

- Uses simple and compound sentences in written compositions
- Uses pronouns, nouns, verbs, adverbs, and adjectives
- Uses conventions of spelling, capitalization, and punctuation (*All lessons where writing or typing a complete sentence option is followed.*)

Uses the general skills and strategies of the reading process

- Establishes and adjusts purposes for reading
- Uses a variety of strategies to extend reading vocabulary
- Uses specific strategies to clear up confusing parts of a text
- Reflects on what has been learned after reading and formulates ideas, opinions, and personal responses to texts

Uses reading skills and strategies to understand a variety of informational texts

- Summarizes and paraphrases information in texts
- Uses new information to adjust and extend personal knowledge base
- Draws conclusions and makes inferences based on explicit and implicit information in texts

What Swallowed Camels

New Words

**These are new words to practice.
Say each word 10 times.**

- located
- gaping
- plate tectonics
- rigid
- slabs
- drift
- magma
- extend

Before or after reading the story, write one sentence that contains at least one new word.

_____
_____
_____
_____

What Swallowed Camels

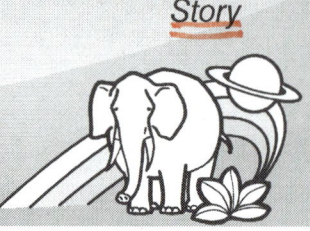

Camels and goats had no warning. They were swallowed alive without any chance of escape. Where, when, why, and how did this happen? The "where" was northern Ethiopia. Ethiopia is a country located on the Horn of Africa. The Horn of Africa, named for its shape, is located on the western side of the African continent. It borders the Indian Ocean. The "when" was September of 2005.

The "how" was that without warning, the earth dropped 10 feet (3 m) and split apart. A gaping, or wide open, hole formed so quickly that the animals were swallowed alive. The gaping hole continued to grow over the next three weeks. The earth quaked over 160 times, and the hole became a crack one-third of a mile (.5 k) long and 25 feet (7.6 m) wide.

Scientists think the "why" has to do with plate tectonics. The theory of plate tectonics states that Earth's crust is made up of moveable plates of rock. There are approximately 15 plates making up Earth's crust. The plates are rigid slabs. The rigid slabs do not bend, but they move. They drift

the Horn of Africa

very slowly, perhaps one to six inches (2.5 to 15 cm) a year. Some slabs drift apart; others drift closer together.

Ethiopia sits on the African plate. The countries on the Arabian Peninsula sit on the Arabian plate. These two plates are drifting apart. As the two plates drift apart, the crust between them weakens. Magma, or hot, melted rock below or within Earth's crust, bubbles up. The huge crack in Ethiopia formed when there was a volcanic explosion of molten rock just a few miles underneath Earth's surface.

Some scientists predict that as the plates continue to drift apart and magma continues to bubble up, the crack will grow much bigger. To the north, it will extend, or stretch, to the Red Sea. To the south, it will extend through the Horn of Africa. The crack will fill with water, cutting the land off from the rest of Africa. In about one million years, the Horn of Africa will become a new continent.

What Swallowed Camels

Quiz

After reading the story, answer the questions. Fill in the circle next to the correct answer.

1. This story is mainly about
   - (a) a crack in Earth's crust.
   - (b) an explosion underneath Ethiopia.
   - (c) camels and goats on the Arabian plate.
   - (d) how Ethiopia will become a new continent.

2. What is not true about the plates that make up Earth's crust?
   - (a) They do not bend.
   - (b) They are rigid slabs.
   - (c) There are approximately 15 of them.
   - (d) They are all drifting away from each other.

3. As the crack becomes bigger, what will it meet up with to the north?
   - (a) magma
   - (b) the Red Sea
   - (c) the Indian Ocean
   - (d) the Arabian Peninsula

4. From the story, one can tell that in one's lifetime
   - (a) one will see a new continent.
   - (b) one will notice the continents drifting.
   - (c) one will not notice the continents drifting.
   - (d) one will see the Arabian plate become a new continent.

5. Think about how the word *gaping* relates to *closed*. Which words relate in the same way?

   gaping : closed
   - (a) rigid : soft
   - (b) quick : fast
   - (c) drifting : moving
   - (d) extended : stretched

©Teacher Created Resources, Inc.   #8037 Nonfiction Reading: Science

Why Mari Said, "No!"

New Words

**These are new words to practice.
Say each word 10 times.**

- element
- unique
- characteristics
- idly

- proposal
- retrieve
- malleable
- dense

Before or after reading the story, write one sentence that contains at least one new word.

_____

_____

_____

_____

Why Mari Said, "No!"

Mari was in the kitchen reviewing for a test on elements. An element is a substance made up of only one type of atom. An atom is the smallest amount of an element that has all the properties of that element. There are over 100 different elements, including carbon, hydrogen, iron, and oxygen. Each element has unique characteristics, or qualities.

Mari looked up from her book. She sat idly, taking a rest from studying. She could hear her father's guest in the living room. The guest was discussing a business proposal, or plan. "This proposal is unique," he said. "It is one of a kind. I propose that we retrieve some gold."

Mari no longer sat idly. She began to take notes on what was being said. "Gold is an amazing element," her father's guest continued. "One of its unique characteristics is that it is malleable. It can be easily shaped. You can beat just one ounce (28 grams) of gold into a thin sheet that measures 300 square feet (27 square meters)!

"I know where there is more than an ounce of gold. I have a map that shows where 500 gold bricks are hidden! The bricks are the usual size, measuring 10.2 x 2.4 x 1.6 in (26 x 6 x 4 cm). My great-great-grandfather hid the gold. He put it in a big cart and covered it with corn. He told people he was going to market. When he came home the next day with his donkey and empty cart, no one knew what he had really done. With your cash investment, we can retrieve the treasure."

Mari had reviewed the characteristics of gold. She knew that it was malleable, but she also knew that it was extremely dense. She wrote a quick note to her father that said, "Gold is extremely dense and very heavy. Just one of your guest's gold bricks would weigh 27 pounds (12 kg)! 500 blocks would weigh 13,500 pounds (6,075 kg)! No donkey could pull that weight! The weight would break the cart! Say 'no' to the proposal!"

Why Mari Said, "No!"

Quiz

After reading the story, answer the questions.
Fill in the circle next to the correct answer.

1. This story is mainly about
   a) Mari and a test.
   b) Mari and a cart.
   c) Mari and an answer.
   ● Mari and an element.

2. What is not a characteristic of gold?
   a) It is dense.
   ● It is a brick.
   c) It is malleable.
   d) It is made from one type of atom.

3. Think about how the word *idle* relates to *resting*. Which words relate in the same way?

   idle : resting

   a) empty : full
   b) heavy : light
   ● thin : slender
   d) unique : common

4. There are two blocks. The blocks are equal size. One block sinks in water. One block floats in water. One reason may be
   ● the block that sinks is denser than the one that floats.
   b) the block that floats is denser than the one that sinks.
   c) the block that sinks is lighter than the one that floats.
   d) the block that floats is heavier than the one that sinks.

5. When gold bricks are carried in armored cars, they are stacked only one deep. Most likely this is to keep
   a) it hidden before it is retrieved.
   b) the gold from being beaten into a thin sheet.
   c) it all from being stolen if the truck is robbed.
   ● the weight of the gold from breaking the axle of the truck.

#8037 Nonfiction Reading: Science   14   ©Teacher Created Resources, Inc.

New Words

The Amazing Jumper

**These are new words to practice.
Say each word 10 times.**

- arthropod
- jointed
- exoskeleton
- thorax
- parasite
- larvae
- cocoons
- pupae

Before or after reading the story, write one sentence that contains at least one new word.

_____

_____

_____

_____

The Amazing Jumper

There is an animal that can jump about 200 times its own body length. If a human could jump an equivalent height, he or she could jump over a skyscraper 40 floors high! What animal has this incredible jumping ability? What makes it possible for this animal to jump such an amazing distance?

The amazing jumper is a flea, a small, wingless insect. Insects are arthropods. Arthropods are creatures with jointed legs. Unlike humans, arthropods do not have inner skeletons. Arthropods possess exoskeletons. An exoskeleton is a hard outer covering. Like all adult insects, a flea has six legs. It has a three-part body made up of a head, a thorax, and an abdomen. Its jointed legs are attached to its thorax, or middle body part.

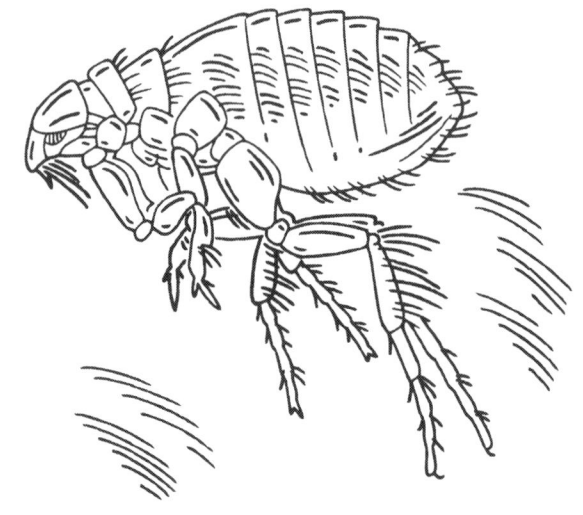

flea

To understand how it is possible for a flea to jump high into the air, it helps to think of a rubber band. When a rubber band is stretched, it contains stored energy. When one lets go of the rubber band, the energy is released. The rubber band flies across the room. Muscles on a flea's long back legs store energy in the same way a stretched rubber band does. When the muscles move, the energy is released in one powerful burst.

Fleas are blood-sucking parasites. A parasite is a plant or animal that lives on or in a host plant or animal. A parasite receives shelter or food from its host but does not provide anything in return. Fleas hatch from eggs laid by mated females. Tiny wormlike larvae that feed on the blood-rich droppings of adult fleas hatch from the eggs.

When fully grown, the larvae pupate. They spin themselves into tiny cocoons, where they change into pupae. The pupae are ready to emerge as adults after six days, but they may wait to break out of their cocoons for six months. This is because a pupa will not emerge until it can leap straight onto a proper host. Pupae use tiny bristles on their legs that can sense heat and movement to know when a proper host is close enough to jump onto.

The Amazing Jumper

Quiz

After reading the story, answer the questions.
Fill in the circle next to the correct answer.

1. Which part of a flea most likely protects it if it falls off of its host onto the ground?
   - a) joints
   - b) thorax
   - c) bristles
   - ● exoskeleton

2. After spinning its cocoon, a pupa may emerge as an adult flea after
   - ● six days
   - b) six months
   - c) seven months
   - d) nine months

3. This story is mainly about
   - a) larvae and cocoons.
   - ● fleas and their legs.
   - c) jumping and rubber bands.
   - d) parasites and their hosts.

4. From the story, one can tell that
   - ● all insects are arthropods.
   - b) some insects have six legs.
   - c) all arthropods are insects.
   - d) some arthropods have jointed legs.

5. Think about how the word *emerge* relates to *hide*. Which words relate in the same way?

   emerge : hide

   - a) sense : feel
   - b) possess : own
   - ● release : store
   - d) prepare : ready

New Words

Conjoined Twins

These are new words to practice.

Say each word 10 times.

- conjoined
- attached
- identical
- embryo

- degrading
- financially
- spectator
- ethical

Before or after reading the story, write one sentence that contains at least one new word.

_____

_____

_____

_____

Conjoined Twins

In about one out of every half-million births, something rare happens: conjoined twins are born. "Conjoined" means joined together, or united. Conjoined twins are physically attached together. Conjoined twins develop from the same egg. Because they develop from the same egg, they are identical. They look the same, are the same sex, and share the same blood type.

An embryo is an animal in the first stages of its growth. With normal identical twins, the embryo cleanly divides between the 13th and 15th days of its development. With conjoined twins, the embryo does not divide entirely. Part of it remains conjoined. Conjoined twins can be attached in a number of ways. Most conjoined twins are female and joined at the chest and abdomen. Some twins are born with two heads and share one two-legged body.

Perhaps the most famous conjoined twins are Eng and Chang. These two brothers were born in 1811 in Thailand. Thailand was called Siam at that time. For this reason, they became known as the Siamese Twins. Some people call all conjoined twins "Siamese twins," but this is incorrect. Today, the term "Siamese twins" is considered degrading. When something is degrading, it shows disrespect.

Eng and Chang

A man named Abel Coffin paid Eng and Chang to come to the United States. Eng and Chang's father had died, and their mother was very poor. The brothers wanted to help their mother financially. Coffin exhibited the twins, charging spectators to view them. Coffin made plenty of money from the thousands of spectators, but Coffin did not treat the brothers well. When the brothers were 21, they were able to free themselves from Coffin. They married two sisters. They lived in two separate houses, each house for three days at a time. They had 21 children between them.

Today, because of medical advances, some conjoined children can be separated. Separating conjoined children brings up ethical, or moral, questions. Is it ethical to separate if one child will be harmed more than the other? What will happen to quality of life? Who should be financially responsible for the high medical costs?

Quiz

Conjoined Twins

After reading the story, answer the questions.
Fill in the circle next to the correct answer.

1. With normal twins, the embryo divides cleanly between the
   a. 13th and 11th day.
   b. 13th and 15th day.
   c. 13th and 19th day.
   d. 13th and 21st day.

2. One should call twins that are physically attached "conjoined"
   a. because it is the ethical term.
   b. because it is the identical term.
   c. because it is the degrading term.
   d. because it is the respectful term.

3. This story is mainly about
   a. Eng and Chang.
   b. embryo development.
   c. a rare type of birth.
   d. ethical questions about conjoined twins.

4. What is not true about most conjoined twins?
   a. They are female.
   b. They have two heads.
   c. They share a two-legged body.
   d. They are attached at the chest and abdomen.

5. Think about how the word *spectator* relates to *watches*. Which words relate in the same way?

   spectator : watches

   a. musician : plays
   b. doctor : hospitals
   c. firefighter : fires
   d. veterinarian : dogs

#8037 Nonfiction Reading: Science   20   ©Teacher Created Resources, Inc.

New Words

Identical Trees

These are new words to practice.
Say each word 10 times.

- grove
- trunks
- quaking
- deciduous

- petioles
- stamen
- pistil
- clone

Before or after reading the story, write one sentence that contains at least one new word.

_____

_____

_____

_____

Identical Trees

Lionel wondered if his eyes were playing a trick on him. It seemed as if every tree in the grove he was looking at had branches growing at identical angles from the trunks. The grove was large. Not all the trees were the same size. How could it be possible that every tree in the grove had branches growing at identical angles from their trunks? What was going on?

Lionel was looking at a grove of quaking aspens. Quaking aspens are deciduous trees. Deciduous trees lose their leaves in the autumn and grow new ones in the spring. Quaking aspen leaves are broad, round, and paper-thin. Its petioles, or leaf stems, are slender and flat. The shape of the leaves and petioles makes it so they catch the wind. The leaves and petioles tremble, quiver, and quake in the slightest breeze.

Quaking aspen trees are male or female. In the spring, male trees produce stamen-bearing flowers. Females produce pistil-bearing flowers. Female trees are fertilized when pollen from male stamens is carried by the wind to the female pistils. Small seeds, covered with fluffy white hairs that help them float in the wind, are produced in the flower pistils.

Very few seeds will develop into seedlings. This is because in order for seeds to grow, they need open, moist soil where they can receive adequate sunlight. For this to occur, the seeds must be carried by the wind to land that is bare and moist. Because there are few moist places bare enough for the seeds to receive adequate sunlight in the forest, aspen trees survive by reproducing in another way, as well.

Aspen trees clone themselves. They make copies that may be younger but contain identical genes. Scientists have studied one aspen in Utah that has 47,000 genetically identical tree trunks! To clone itself, an aspen sends out new shoots, or suckers. The suckers spring up from buds on the aspen's shallow root system. The young tree has an excellent chance of survival because it is nourished and watered by the fully formed root system of the parent tree.

Quiz

Identical Trees

After reading the story, answer the questions.
Fill in the circle next to the correct answer.

1. Pollen is produced by the
   - (a) seeds.
   - (b) genes.
   - (c) pistils.
   - **(d) stamens.**

2. This story is mainly about
   - (a) clones.
   - (b) a grove.
   - **(c) aspen trees.**
   - (d) branch angles.

3. Which statement is false?
   - (a) Quaking aspen petioles are slender.
   - (b) All quaking aspen seeds need sunlight.
   - (c) Quaking aspen seeds have fluffy hairs.
   - **(d) All quaking aspens have identical genes.**

4. Think about how the word *trunk* relates to *branch*. Which words relate in the same way?

   | trunk : branch |

   - (a) eye : see
   - **(b) body : arm**
   - (c) leg : pants
   - (d) hand : foot

5. Quaking aspens are often knocked over in high winds. One reason may be that
   - (a) they have deep root systems.
   - **(b) they have shallow root systems.**
   - (c) they have identical root systems.
   - (d) they have fully formed root systems.

©Teacher Created Resources, Inc.   23   #8037 Nonfiction Reading: Science

New Words

The Extreme Sport of Paper-Folding

These are new words to practice.

Say each word 10 times.

- issued
- varying
- spur
- origami
- recreation
- extreme
- participants
- complex

Before or after reading the story, write one sentence that contains at least one new word.

_____
_____
_____
_____

The Extreme Sport of Paper-Folding

The challenge was issued or sent out. The challenge was to produce an Eupatorus beetle. Eupatorus beetles, more commonly known as rhinoceros beetles, have five horns of varying, or different, lengths on their heads. They have six knees. Each knee joint has a spur. The spurs are like tiny spines that stick straight up. The beetles' toes are delicate and complicated.

Who was being challenged to produce a rhinoceros beetle that included its horns of varying lengths, its spurs, and its toes? The challenge was issued to people who fold paper. Origami is the Japanese art of folding paper. Most often, origami is done for recreation, or fun. For some paper-folders, origami is more than light recreation. It is an extreme sport. It is a sport that pushes paper-folding to the greatest degree.

Participants of the extreme sport of paper-folding must follow two rules. The first rule the participants must follow is that they can only use one piece of square paper. The second rule is that the paper cannot be cut or torn in any way. Most origami creations take about 20 steps. Complex creations, such as the rhinoceros beetle, take well over 100.

Designing origami patterns is a hard and complex task. One man who has published a book of patterns is Satoshi Kamiya. Kamiya once folded a dragon with overlapping scales. The dragon was coiled and rearing. Its teeth were triangular and sharp. Its hands were tiny, grasping claws. Kamiya said that he saw the finished dragon in his mind. Then, he unfolded it, one piece at a time.

Dr. Robert Lang was a scientist who worked with lasers and folded paper for fun. Today, Lang's origami is more than recreational. It is a full-time job. Lang has used his origami skills to work out how a car's airbag can be folded into a steering column. He has designed a telescope lens that was packed into a nine-foot (2.7 meter) cylinder and could be shot into space. The lens was the size of a football field when it was unfolded.

Quiz

The Extreme Sport of Paper-Folding

After reading the story, answer the questions.
Fill in the circle next to the correct answer.

1. This story is mainly about
   a) extreme sports.
   b) the art of paper-folding.
   c) what some people do for recreation.
   d) Satoshi Kamiya and Dr. Robert Lang.

2. What did Kamiya do first when he made his dragon?
   a) folded the paper
   b) unfolded the pattern
   c) made a pattern with fold lines
   d) saw the finished dragon in his mind

3. Think about how the word *complex* relates to *easy*. Which words relate in the same way?

   | complex : easy |

   a) torn : ripped
   b) varying : alike
   c) recreational : fun
   d) finished : complete

4. How many knees does a rhinoceros beetle have?
   a) 2
   b) 4
   c) 6
   d) 8

5. Joe was _a participant_ in the jump-rope contest.
   a) a spur
   b) an extreme
   c) a participant
   d) an overlapping

New Words

What Was Not a Grave

**These are new words to practice.
Say each word 10 times.**

- mounds
- constructed
- unique
- incubating
- regulates
- vegetation
- debris
- maintained

Before or after reading the story, write one sentence that contains at least one new word.

_____
_____
_____
_____

©Teacher Created Resources, Inc.   27   #8037 Nonfiction Reading: Science

What Was Not a Grave

Early European explorers were finding mound after mound on the Australian continent. The mounds were carefully constructed. Many of the mounds were over 3.3 feet (1 m) high. They were over 13.1 feet (4 m) wide. The explorers were sure they were finding carefully constructed graves. What else could the gigantic mounds be?

The mounds were not graves. They were malleefowl nests! Malleefowl are large birds that have a unique way of incubating their eggs. Malleefowl do not sit on their eggs. Instead, they use their nest, or mound, to incubate the eggs. This unique way of incubating eggs is possible because of the way the mounds are constructed. It is possible because the male carefully regulates, or controls, the temperature of the nest.

To construct a nest, the birds spend hours piling soil, sand, and wet vegetation litter into a large mound. Vegetation litter is plant debris, or garbage. After the nest is constructed, the female lays about 20 eggs in a deep hole in the mound's top. The male covers the eggs with mound material as soon as they are laid.

The direct heat of the sun incubates the eggs, as does heat from the nest. The heat from the nest comes from the wet vegetation. As the plant debris rots, it gives off heat. The temperature inside the nest must be maintained, or kept, at about 91.4°F (33°C). It is believed that the male checks the nest temperature with his tongue when he sticks his bill deep into the nest.

If the rotting litter gives off too much heat, the male regulates the temperature by digging a hole in the mound and allowing heat to escape. When enough heat has escaped, he fills the hole with cool sand. If the sun's heat is too great, the male adds protective layers of sand that absorb the heat. Depending on the season, the male will remove sand and soil to cool or warm it by spreading it on the ground. Nest temperature is maintained by the constant removal and replacement of cooled and heated sand and soil.

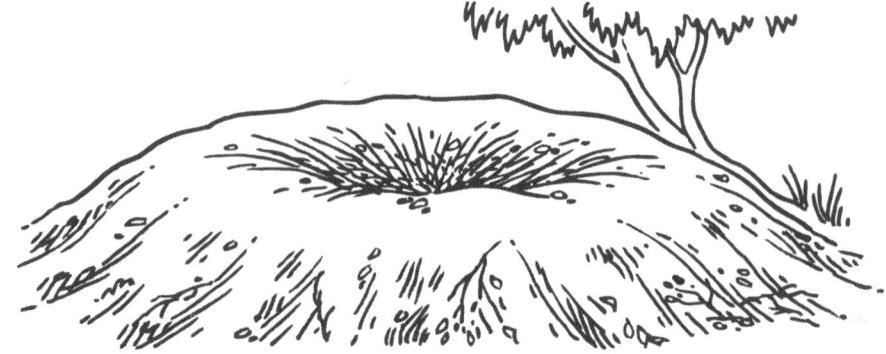

What Was Not a Grave

Quiz

After reading the story, answer the questions.
Fill in the circle next to the correct answer.

1. It is believed that the male malleefowl checks the temperature of the nest
   a) with its tongue.
   b) by regulating it.
   c) with protective layers of sand.
   d) by digging holes to allow heat to escape.

2. From the story, one can tell that European explorers most likely
   a) checked the nest temperature.
   b) had not seen nests like this before.
   c) were worried about protecting graves.
   d) would have eaten the eggs if they had found them.

3. This story is mainly about
   a) what European explorers found.
   b) where and how many eggs malleefowls lay.
   c) how malleefowls construct nests and incubate eggs.
   d) why the nests of Australian birds look like graves.

4. If the rotting vegetation gives off too much heat, the male
   a) digs a hole in the nest.
   b) adds protective layers of sand.
   c) maintains the temperature constantly.
   d) removes soil and spreads it on the ground to cool.

5. Think about how the word *debris* relates to *litter*. Which words relate in the same way?

   debris : litter

   a) wet : dry
   b) cool : warm
   c) unique : common
   d) gigantic : large

©Teacher Created Resources, Inc.   29   #8037 Nonfiction Reading: Science

New Words

A Town That Gets No Sun

These are new words to practice.

Say each word 10 times.

- founded
- steep
- site
- plundered

- inhabitants
- declining
- heliostats
- diffuse

Before or after reading the story, write one sentence that contains at least one new word.

_____

_____

_____

_____

A Town That Gets No Sun

Rattenberg is a tiny village. It was founded over 600 years, or six centuries, ago. It was founded in Austria, a country in Europe. It is located in the bottom of a steep-sided mountain valley. It is nestled between the Inn River and steep mountain walls. The original site was chosen for safety reasons. The river and the mountains were natural barriers. They provided a natural defense. They helped to protect the village from being raided and plundered, or robbed with force.

Today the inhabitants of Rattenberg are not concerned about raids. They have no fears of being plundered. The inhabitants have a completely different concern. They are worried about the village's declining population. People are leaving. The village is safe from raiders, so why is the village's population declining?

There is a lack of sunlight in Rattenberg. During the cold winter months, the village is in shadow. Blocked by the high mountains, the sun stays below the horizon. The horizon is the line where the sky seems to meet the earth. People do not want to live where there are months of dark shadow. Young people are choosing home sites where there is sunlight.

The inhabitants of Rattenberg have come up with a solution. They are going to light their village with heliostats, giant rotating mirrors. Fifteen heliostats will be placed in a sunny field across the Inn River. The mirrors will be set on poles. Each mirror will measure about six feet (1.8 m) across. The mirrors will be programmed to track the sun. The mirrors will reflect light to a mirror-covered tower. The tower site is located next to an ancient stone fort that was used to help protect the village long ago.

The mirrors on the tower will reflect light to smaller mirrors placed on village buildings. The smaller mirrors will do two things. First, they will reflect the light down the village streets. Second, they will diffuse the light. When something is diffused, it is spread out. It is not as centered. Diffused light will help to prevent glare. Diffused light will lessen the risk of fire.

A Town That Gets No Sun

Quiz

After reading the story, answer the questions.
Fill in the circle next to the correct answer.

1. How many heliostats does the village of Rattenberg plan on using?
   a) 13
   b) 14
   c) 15
   d) 16

2. From the story one can tell that in Rattenberg
   a) people need to protect themselves from raiders.
   b) people are choosing home sites with reflected light.
   c) the horizon would be lower if there were no mountains.
   d) the sun rises higher than the horizon during the winter.

3. This story is mainly about
   a) heliostats.
   b) a town in Austria.
   c) declining populations.
   d) using mirrors for light.

4. From the story, one can tell that a century is
   a) 10 years
   b) 100 years
   c) 1,000 years
   d) 10,000 years

5. Think about how the word *diffused* relates to *centered*. Which words relate in the same way?

   diffused : centered

   a) founded : ended
   b) plundered : robbed
   c) declined : lessoned
   d) concerned : worried

New Words

45,000 Years of Penguin Droppings

These are new words to practice.
Say each word 10 times.

- retreated
- current
- exposed
- excavated
- preserved
- guano
- absorb
- carbon 14

Before or after reading the story, write one sentence that contains at least one new word.

_____

_____

_____

_____

45,000 Years of Penguin Droppings

A huge sheet of ice covers the continent of Antarctica. The sheet's size has changed over millions of years. It has retreated and gotten smaller. It has advanced and gotten bigger. Scientists are very interested in the current, or present, size of the ice sheet. They know it is retreating. The coastline is changing. Land that was previously covered by ice is becoming exposed, or seen. One scientist has found a way to measure when some of this land was last exposed. How is this possible?

The scientist studied Adélie penguin waste. Adélie penguins nest in large colonies, or groups. Sometimes colonies nest on the same site for thousands of years. The birds nest only on ice-free terrain, or land. They construct their nests with small beach pebbles. By studying ancient nesting sites, the scientist could tell when land had been exposed by retreating ice.

First, the scientist excavated, or dug up, nesting sites. Both old and current sites were excavated. Antarctica's climate is cold and dry. Because of its climate, the penguin's waste was preserved. It did not rot away. Layers of guano, or droppings, built up over thousands of years. Feathers, skin, bones, and even whole chicks were preserved in the layers of guano.

The scientist took the droppings and carbon dated them. All living things contain carbon. Plants absorb carbon from the atmosphere. Animals absorb carbon when they eat plants or animals that eat plants. Living things stop absorbing carbon when they die. Scientists know how long carbon 14, one type of carbon, takes to decay. Carbon 14 is radioactive. It decays at a steady rate. By measuring the amount of carbon 14 an object contains, scientists can estimate its age.

The scientist was able to date nesting sites from penguin droppings for the last 45,000 years. Using layer site dates, he could tell when the ice sheet retreated and advanced. He found that the most active Adélie nesting site is 2,000 years old. He found that two cold periods 5,000 to 4,000 and 2,000 to 1,100 years ago forced Adélie penguins to find new sites.

45,000 Years of Penguin Droppings

Quiz

After reading the story, answer the questions.
Fill in the circle next to the correct answer.

1. This story is mainly about
   a. the way carbon dating works.
   b. a scientist who measured carbon 14 in penguins.
   c. using guano to find when ice retreated and advanced.
   d. where and how Adélie penguins construct their nests.

2. Carbon dating would not work if
   a. all living things contained carbon.
   b. carbon 14 did not decay at a steady rate.
   c. Antarctica's cold, dry climate did not preserve guano.
   d. the amount of carbon 14 could be measured in an object.

3. When the Adélie penguins were forced to find new nesting sites 5,000 to 4,000 years ago it was because
   a. the ice had advanced.
   b. guano layers built up.
   c. the ice had retreated.
   d. the site was excavated.

4. What is not listed as being preserved in layers or guano?
   a. eggs
   b. skin
   c. chicks
   d. feathers

5. Think about how the word *retreat* relates to *advance*. Which words relate in the same way?

   | retreat : advance |

   a. expose : show
   b. preserve : rot
   c. date : ancient
   d. absorb : measure

©Teacher Created Resources, Inc.   35   #8037 Nonfiction Reading: Science

New Words

Finding the Counterfeit Coin

These are new words to practice.

Say each word 10 times.

- require
- aid
- assistance
- conundrum
- identical
- counterfeit
- scale
- balance

Before or after reading the story, write one sentence that contains at least one new word.

_____

_____

_____

_____

Finding the Counterfeit Coin

"Help, help!" said Ms. Henderson. "I require your aid and assistance! I am faced with a conundrum. A conundrum is like a difficult riddle. It is a puzzle that seems impossible to solve. Would you please help me solve this difficult conundrum?" The students were quick to offer their aid and assistance. They were ready to try and solve any conundrum put before them.

Ms. Henderson said, "These gold coins look identical, but one of these coins is counterfeit. It is not real. The counterfeit coin looks identical to the others, but it is slightly heavier. We only have a scale balance in this room. Our scale balance is about to break. At most, we can use it two times. My conundrum is this: how can I find out which coin is counterfeit using only a scale balance two times?"

The students discussed the problem. They came up with an answer. "Ms. Henderson," the students said, "We can provide aid and assistance. We can solve your conundrum. We require nothing more than the use of the scale balance two times. First, divide the coins into three even piles with three coins each. Second, put two of the piles on the scale—three coins on one side, three coins on the other.

"If one side is heavier, the counterfeit coin will be in the pile on the heavier side. Next, place two of the coins from the heavier pile on the scale, one on each side. If the scale balances, the counterfeit coin is the one you did not put on the scale. If one side is heavier, it is the counterfeit coin.

"If the first two piles you placed on the scale balanced, then the counterfeit coin is in the remaining pile. Simply try and balance two of the coins in the remaining pile. If they balance, the remaining coin is counterfeit. If one is heavier, it is the counterfeit coin. The conundrum is solved!" The students had done it! By balancing coins just two times, they were able to provide Ms. Henderson with the information she required!

Finding the Counterfeit Coin

After reading the story, answer the questions.
Fill in the circle next to the correct answer.

1. This story is mainly about
   a) what a conundrum is.
   b) the students who gave assistance.
   c) balancing coins to solve a conundrum.
   d) Ms. Henderson and her counterfeit coins.

2. From the story, one can tell that a scale balance can tell one
   a) the weight of an object.
   b) if two objects are the same weight.
   c) the weight of an counterfeit object.
   d) how much more one object weighs than the other.

3. Think about how the word *counterfeit* relates to *real*. Which words relate in the same way?

   counterfeit : real

   a) balanced : even
   b) assistance : help
   c) conundrum : puzzle
   d) identical : different

4. How many coins would the students put on each side of the scale the second time they used it?
   a) 1
   b) 2
   c) 3
   d) 4

5. If the first two piles of coins placed on the scale balanced, then the students would know that the counterfeit coin
   a) was heavier than the other coins.
   b) was one of the coins on the scale.
   c) was in the third pile not on the scale.
   d) was identical to the rest of the coins.

New Words

Amphibian Escort

These are new words to practice.

Say each word 10 times.

* amphibians
* larvae
* salamanders
* emerge

* habitat
* dormant
* migrate
* escort

Before or after reading the story, write one sentence that contains at least one new word.

_____

_____

_____

_____

Amphibian Escort

It was the first warm rainy night of spring. Instead of being told to get ready for bed, Will was told, "Get your rain gear on. Arm yourself with a flashlight. You're not going to crawl into your snug, dry bed tonight. You are going to save hundreds of lives." Will was only a student. Whose lives could Will save, and how could he save them?

Amphibians are cold-blooded animals with backbones. Amphibians live both on land and in water. They are animals whose larvae, or immature forms, have gills. Their adult forms have lungs. Frogs and salamanders are amphibians. Their larvae have gills, while their mature adult forms have lungs.

Will lived in a part of the eastern state of Vermont where, on the first warm rainy night of spring, frogs and salamanders would emerge, or come out, from their winter habitat of upland forest. During the winter, the frogs and salamanders had remained mostly dormant. When something is dormant it is not actively moving or growing. After emerging, thousands of frogs and salamanders would migrate down to pools in lowland swamps where they would mate.

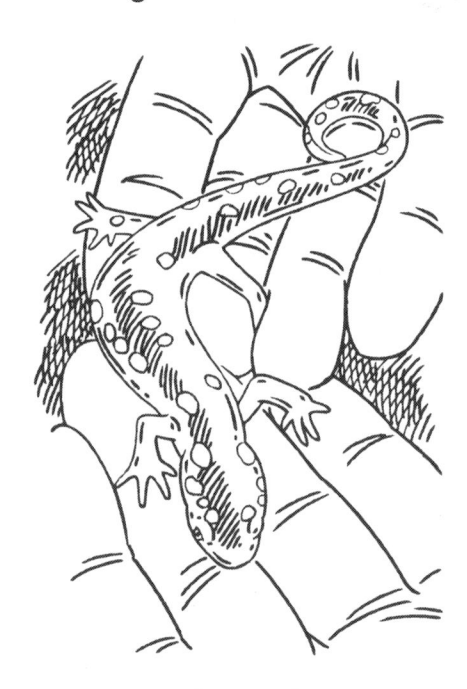

salamander

Will could save the lives of hundreds of these migrating amphibians by a simple act. He could escort, or accompany, them along part of their migration route. Why would animals that had survived for so long need an escort on part of their migration route? Why would these animals need a person to accompany them? A road had been constructed between the amphibians' winter and spring habitats. Will and other volunteers were needed to help stop the amphibians from being flattened by passing cars.

During the long night, Will helped to patrol about 200 yards (183 meters) of road. Will carefully scanned the road with his flashlight. When he spotted an amphibian, he would gently pick up the moist creature in his hands and deposit it down on the other side of the road. Will kept a count of the number and kinds of amphibians he escorted so that scientists could track population numbers.

Amphibian Escort

Quiz

After reading the story, answer the questions.
Fill in the circle next to the correct answer.

1. What is not true about amphibians?
   - a) They have backbones.
   - **b) They are warm-blooded.**
   - c) Their larvae have gills.
   - d) They live both on land and in water.

2. This story is mainly about
   - a) what an amphibian is.
   - b) amphibian volunteers.
   - c) migrating amphibians.
   - **d) helping some amphibians.**

3. A volcano that has not erupted for years is said to be
   - **a) dormant.**
   - b) emerging.
   - c) an escort.
   - d) migrating.

4. Think about how the word *mature* relates to *immature*. Which words relate in the same way?

   mature : immature

   - **a) moist : dry**
   - b) simple : easy
   - c) dormant : still
   - d) flattened : squashed

5. From the story, one can tell that
   - a) amphibians only migrate in Vermont.
   - b) Will did not think he could save lives.
   - c) animals often change their migration routes.
   - **d) a road may affect animal population numbers.**

New Words

Blisters—To Pop or Not

**These are new words to practice.
Say each word 10 times.**

- organ
- fluids
- keratin
- epidermis

- dermis
- plasma
- exposing
- bacteria

**Before or after reading the story, write one sentence
that contains at least one new word.**

_____

_____

_____

_____

Blisters—To Pop or Not

Tom burned himself on a hot cookie sheet. Blisters formed on the ends of his fingers where they had come in contact with the sheet. Tom wondered why the blisters developed and what exactly they were filled with. He wondered if he should pop them.

The answers to Tom's questions start with understanding the largest organ of our bodies: our skin. Our skin is a sense organ that makes up about 15 percent of our body weight. It is the first line of defense against illness because it prevents most germs and chemicals from entering and infecting our bodies. It keeps fluids inside and protects the body from drying out.

Our skin is made up of billions of tiny cells. The top, outermost layer is made up of dead cells. The cells are made mostly of a protein called keratin. Two layers of living skin cells, the epidermis and the dermis, are underneath the thick, protective keratin layer. The epidermis is directly below the keratin, and it is about as thick as a sheet of paper. The dermis, making up about 90% of our skin's thickness, lies below the epidermis. The dermis contains oil and sweat glands, hair follicles, nerve endings, and blood vessels.

When Tom touched the hot cookie sheet, the heat damaged and killed living skin cells. It caused skin layers to separate. The damaged skin cells sent out chemicals that caused a clear fluid in the blood called plasma to leak out of nearby blood vessels. Some plasma leaked into body tissues, making it swell. Some plasma seeped into gaps between separated skin layers and formed bubble-like blisters.

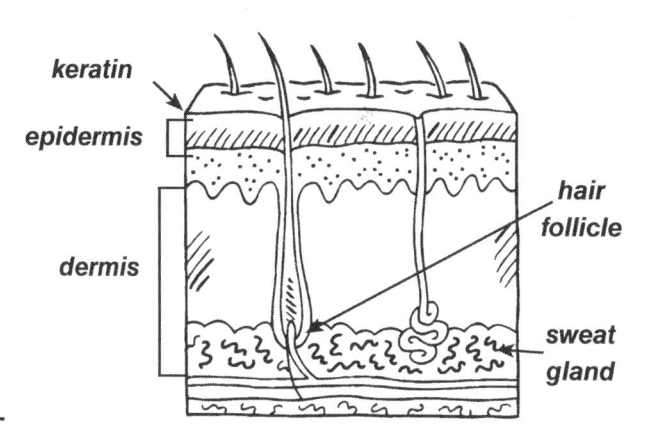

A blister should not be popped. A blister protects ones skin from further damage just as a scab protects ones skin while a wound heals. If Tom popped his blisters, he would be exposing his damaged skin to bacteria. Exposure to bacteria may cause infection. Left alone, Tom's blisters will get smaller as the tissue underneath heals and the plasma seeps back into the tissue. As for the outer dead part, it will simply peel off over time.

Quiz

Blisters—To Pop or Not

After reading the story, answer the questions.
Fill in the circle next to the correct answer.

1. The thickest part of our skin is the
   - a) cells
   - **b) dermis** ✓
   - c) keratin
   - d) epidermis

2. A blister is formed when
   - a) skin is exposed to bacteria.
   - b) chemicals cause the tissue to swell.
   - **c) plasma seeps into gaps between skin layers.** ✓
   - d) tissue underneath the outermost layer heals.

3. This story is mainly about
   - a) skin layers.
   - b) Tom and a hot sheet.
   - **c) an organ and blisters.** ✓
   - d) the first line of defense.

4. A scratch that extends down to the epidermis does not bleed because
   - **a) blood vessels are only in the dermis.** ✓
   - b) the keratin layer is made of dead cells.
   - c) the open wound is not exposed to bacteria.
   - d) plasma leaks into the tissue and makes it swell.

5. Think about how the word *expose* relates to *cover*. Which words relate in the same way?

   expose : cover

   - **a) enter : exit** ✓
   - b) damage : harm
   - c) contain : hold
   - d) defend : protect

#8037 Nonfiction Reading: Science   44   ©Teacher Created Resources, Inc.

The World's First Life Preserver

These are new words to practice.
Say each word 10 times.

- civilization
- archeologist
- ancient
- tablet
- preserved
- resin
- leather
- tannin

Before or after reading the story, write one sentence that contains at least one new word.

_____
_____
_____
_____

The World's First Life Preserver

More than 8,000 years ago, people began to settle in Mesopotamia. One of the world's first civilizations developed in this ancient land. Mesopotamia means "between the rivers." It was a triangular piece of land located between the Tigris and Euphrates rivers. It was located in what is now part of present day Syria, Turkey, and Iraq. Civilization is the stage in human progress when arts, science, and government were developed.

Archeologists study archeology. Archeology is the study of ancient times and people. Ancient Mesopotamians developed a system of writing. They recorded information on clay tablets. Information about the Mesopotamians has been preserved, or kept, through time, on the tablets. Archeologists have learned how to read the clay tablets. Some of the tablets discussed science. By studying the tablets, archeologists have been able to follow ancient scientific developments.

First, people learned how to use oils. The oils came from sheep, birds, and fish. They came from nuts and seeds, too. About 5,000 years ago, people made the first soap using vegetable oils. They used oils to light lamps and torches. They used oils to make medicines. Oils were combined with wool and resin and used to seal ships' hulls, or bodies. Resin is a sticky substance that oozes out of certain plants and trees.

People went on to use oils in the production of the ancient civilization's first leather. Leather is material made from tanned animal skins. First, the people soaked the skins with tannin. Tannin preserved the skin and kept it from rotting. Gall nuts, tree bark, and pomegranate rinds were part of the tannin solution. Second, the skins were rubbed with fats and oils until they were soft.

Inventions for ways to use leather were recorded on the tablets. Leather was used for harnesses and sandals. It was used to make pouches. The pouches were for milk, water, and butter. Leather was even used to make what might be the world's first life preserver! Leather pouches were filled with air. The air-filled pouches were used as floats! They were used to help swimmers safely get across rivers.

The World's First Life Preserver

Quiz

After reading the story, answer the questions.
Fill in the circle next to the correct answer.

1. What was the tannin used for in the production of leather?
   a) to seal ships' hulls
   b) to preserve the skins ✓
   c) to keep the skins soft
   d) to mix gall nuts, tree bark, and pomegranate rinds

2. From the story, one can tell that
   a) ancient Mesopotamians did not know how to swim.
   b) archeologists are mainly interested in science.
   c) people in ancient Mesopotamia knew how to make butter. ✓
   d) ships were invented after people learned how to use oil.

3. This story is mainly about ✓
   a) a life preserver.
   b) how leather is made.
   c) archeology in Mesopotamia.
   d) some ancient scientific developments.

4. Ancient Mesopotamia was part of what present-day country?
   a) Iran
   b) Iraq ✓
   c) Spain
   d) Sudan

5. Think about how the word *float* relates to *sink*. Which words relate in the same way?

   float : sink

   a) combine : mix ✓
   b) produce : make
   c) preserve : rot
   d) civilize : develop

100

©Teacher Created Resources, Inc. 47 #8037 Nonfiction Reading: Science

New Words

What Is It?

**These are new words to practice.
Say each word 10 times.**

- classification
- kingdom
- phylum
- class
- order
- family
- genus
- species

Before or after reading the story, write one sentence that contains at least one new word.

_____

_____

_____

_____

What Is It?

Your feet stink! You are told that you suffer from what is commonly known as "athlete's foot." What exactly is athlete's foot? Athlete's foot is caused by a parasite. A parasite feeds on other living things without providing anything useful in return. Is this parasite an animal or plant? Where does it fit in the order of living things?

Classification systems arrange groups according to similarities and differences. They arrange things into categories. One common classification system uses these categories: Kingdom, Phylum, Class, Order, Family, Genus, and Species. Kingdom is the most general category. Species is the most specific category. It has been estimated that there are more than 10 million different species of living things on Earth.

Human beings, for example, are part of the animal kingdom. They belong to the phylum Chordates. They belong to the class Mammal. They belong to the Primate order. They belong to the genus *Homo*. They belong to the species *Homo sapiens*. Only people are *Homo sapiens*. The sentence, "King Philip Came Over For Good Spaghetti" can be used to help one remember category names and order. The first letter of each word in the sentence is the first letter of each one of the categories.

Today many scientists use a classification system with five kingdoms. The members of each kingdom share similar features. One kingdom is the animal kingdom. Insects, amphibians, reptiles, and birds are all part of the animal kingdom. So are worms and mollusks. One kingdom is the plant kingdom. Mosses and ferns are part of this kingdom. So are conifers and flowering plants.

One kingdom is the protist kingdom. Plantlike algae belong to this kingdom, as do animal-like protozoa. Fungus-like slime molds do, too. One kingdom is the monera kingdom. Single-celled organisms belong to this kingdom. One kingdom is the fungi kingdom. Mushrooms, molds, and yeasts are part of this kingdom. Athlete's foot is not a plant or animal. It is not a protist or monera. It is a fungus. It belongs to the fungi kingdom.

What Is It?

Quiz

After reading the story, answer the questions.
Fill in the circle next to the correct answer.

1. This story is mainly about
   - (a) putting living things in categories.
   - (b) what category parasites are part of.
   - (c) how to remember classification categories.
   - (d) what kingdom, phylum, class, order, family, genus, and species people are in.

2. In the sentence "King Philip Came Over For Good Spaghetti," the word *for* is used to help one remember what category?
   - (a) class
   - (b) phylum
   - (c) family
   - (d) species

3. Which category below is the most general?
   - (a) genus
   - (b) order
   - (c) phylum
   - (d) family

4. What is not an example of a classification system?
   - (a) books arranged by subject
   - (b) a line for a roller coaster ride
   - (c) meat and fruit sections in grocery stores
   - (d) names listed alphabetically in a phone book

5. Think about how the word *mold* relates to *fungi*. Which words relate in the same way?

   mold : fungi

   - (a) bird : monera
   - (b) moss : protist
   - (c) fern : protozoa
   - (d) mollusk : animal

#8037 Nonfiction Reading: Science ©Teacher Created Resources, Inc.

New Words

Getting Stung on Purpose

These are new words to practice.

Say each word 10 times.

- anemone
- invertebrate
- tentacles
- nematocysts

- poisonous
- paralyze
- immunity
- predator

Before or after reading the story, write one sentence that contains at least one new word.

_____
_____
_____
_____

Getting Stung on Purpose

A sea anemone may look like a flower, but it is an animal. It is an invertebrate. An invertebrate is an animal without a backbone. People mistake sea anemones for flowers because of the way the creature anchors itself to the ocean floor and its colorful tentacles. A sea anemone's tentacles are long, slender parts. They grow around the anemone's mouth. They wave back and forth in the water.

A sea anemone's tentacles may look pretty, but they are deadly to most fish. This is because the tentacles contain nematocysts. Nematocysts are stinging cells. If a fish swims around an anemone's tentacles, it will get stung. The poisonous stings will paralyze or kill the fish. When something is paralyzed, it cannot move. The paralyzed or dead fish will then become the anemone's meal. The anemone will use its tentacles to carry its meal to its mouth.

The clown fish uses the sea anemone for safety. The fish hides among its tentacles. Why doesn't the clown fish die from the anemone's poisonous stings? The clown fish does not die because it gets stung on purpose! First, the clown fish swims around the anemone's tentacles. It does not touch them. Then, it begins to touch them every so slightly.

As the clown fish carefully darts in and out of the tentacles, it slowly builds up immunity to the anemone's stings. The fish becomes protected from the anemone's poisons. A clown fish's immunity does not last forever. If a clown fish leaves its anemone for more than one hour, it will no longer be immune. It will have to be stung all over again to build up its immunity.

What happens if a fish swims to another anemone? The immunity to one anemone does not cross over to another anemone. The fish will have to be stung again! It will have to develop immunity to the new anemone's poison. When the immune fish is safe swimming in the anemone's tentacles, it is also safe from its predators! The anemone's poisonous tentacles will kill predators that would ordinarily eat the clown fish!

Quiz

Getting Stung on Purpose

After reading the story, answer the questions.
Fill in the circle next to the correct answer.

1. How long can a clown fish stay away from its anemone before losing its immunity?
   - (a) 15 minutes
   - (b) 30 minutes
   - (c) 45 minutes
   - **(d) 60 minutes**

2. Which animal is an invertebrate?
   - **(a) a slug**
   - (b) a mouse
   - (c) a whale
   - (d) a person

3. This story is mainly about
   - (a) immunity from sea anemones.
   - (b) sea anemones and predators.
   - **(c) clown fish and sea anemones.**
   - (d) a sea anemone's poisonous tentacles.

4. Why might it be good for a sea anemone to have a clown fish swimming among its tentacles?
   - (a) The sea anemone can paralyze and eat the clown fish.
   - (b) The clown fish can sting the sea anemone's predators.
   - (c) The clown fish is protected by the immunity it builds up.
   - **(d) The predators that come to eat the clown fish are stung and eaten by the anemone.**

5. Think about how the word *immune* relates to *protected*. Which words relate in the same way?

   | immune : protected |

   - (a) left : stay
   - (b) alive : killed
   - **(c) wrong : mistaken**
   - (d) move : paralyzed

A Season for Potholes

These are new words to practice.

Say each word 10 times.

- expectations
- potholes
- mild
- vehicle
- seep
- expand
- thaws
- cavity

Before or after reading the story, write one sentence that contains at least one new word.

_____

_____

_____

_____

Story

A Season for Potholes

Ms. Park said, "It is now late winter. Spring is near. Tell me what you expect to spring up now that one season is ending and a new one is beginning." Ms. Park started a list on the board of the student's expectations. The list included Rosa and Frank's expectations of "warmer days" and "more sunlight hours." It included Dan and Lilia's expectations of "early blooming flowers like crocuses" and "migrating birds returning from the south." The list also included Nika's expectations of "more potholes."

Robert was new to the class. He had moved from a warm place where the change in seasons was mild. Living in the Midwest, where the differences between seasons were extreme, was new to him. Robert said, "I don't understand why 'more potholes' is on the list. I thought all potholes were tied to the number of vehicles on the road. Why would one expect more potholes now that winter is ending? Is there a season where more potholes spring up?"

Ms. Park said, "Near the end of winter, the days often warm up above freezing temperatures. Snow and ice melt, turning to water. The water seeps through cracks in road surfaces and gets under the pavement. At night, temperatures drop. The water under the road that seeped through the surface cracks freezes. As the water freezes, it expands and takes up more space. The expanding ice pushes the pavement up and the subsurface down.

"The ice that formed during the night thaws during the warmer day temperatures. When the ice melts, a cavity, or hole, is left under the pavement. When a heavy vehicle like a car or truck drives over the cavity, the pavement cracks and breaks. A pothole springs up!"

Robert said, "Now I understand. Late winter and early spring can seem like 'pothole season.' This is because repeated nighttime freezes and daytime thaws are more likely to create conditions for potholes to develop. In places with milder temperatures where repeated freezing and thawing is less common, potholes occur for different reasons."

Quiz

A Season for Potholes

After reading the story, answer the questions.
Fill in the circle next to the correct answer.

1. Why is there a cavity left when the ice under the road thaws?

   a) Ice takes up more space than water.
   b) Differences in the seasons are extreme.
   c) Water that seeps under the road freezes at night.
   d) Heavy vehicles cause the pavement to crack and break.

2. This story is mainly about

   a) freezing and thawing.
   b) late winter and early spring.
   c) Ms. Park and the list she made.
   d) when and why some potholes form.

3. What is not listed as a student's expectation?

   a) more sunlight hours
   b) melting snow and ice
   c) early blooming flowers like crocuses
   d) migrating birds returning from the south

4. Think about how the word *crocus* relates to *flower*. Which words relate in the same way?

   crocus : flower

   a) bird : south
   b) car : vehicle
   c) winter : freeze
   d) student : teacher

5. If temperatures are below freezing day *and* night, potholes are less likely to develop because

   a) there is no daytime thawing.
   b) there are less vehicles on the roads.
   c) there are extreme differences between seasons.
   d) there is water seeping below the road surface.

#8037 Nonfiction Reading: Science

The True Story Behind DNA

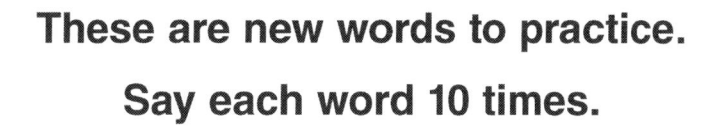

These are new words to practice.

Say each word 10 times.

- DNA
- genes
- characteristics
- helix
- vital
- lecture
- structure
- data

Before or after reading the story, write one sentence that contains at least one new word.

_____

_____

_____

_____

The True Story Behind DNA

DNA is short for deoxyribonucleic acid. DNA is in every plant and animal. DNA contains our genes. Our genes carry our genetic information. Parents pass on characteristics to their children through their genes. Characteristics like hair, eye, and skin color are all due to the genes we inherit from our parents.

The DNA molecule is in the shape of a double helix. A helix is a shape like a spiral. DNA is two helixes, linked together. James Watson and Francis Crick are given credit for discovering DNA's shape in 1953. The two men were awarded a Nobel Prize for their work. The truth is that another scientist paid a vital, or key, role in the discovery. The scientist was a woman named Rosalind Franklin.

Franklin was born in London, England in 1920. She became a scientist at a time when this was highly unusual for women. Franklin was not treated equally. For example, Franklin was not allowed into the place where the men ate lunch because she was a woman. She was left out of scientific discussions. Ideas were not shared.

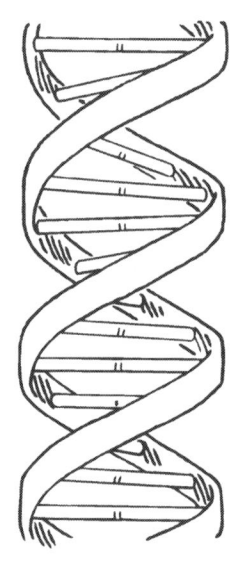

DNA molecule

Rosalind Franklin

Franklin found a way to photograph a form of DNA. In November 1951, Franklin gave a lecture, or talk, to fellow researchers. Watson was in the audience. In her lecture, Franklin mentioned that she believed DNA's structure was a helix. Watson was excited and shared Franklin's ideas with Crick. The two men then showed Franklin a DNA model they had made. Franklin pointed out the model's basic mistakes. Franklin, meanwhile, continued to collect data, or information, and develop ways to improve her DNA photographs. Her data and photographs proved that DNA was a helix.

Franklin did not know it, but Watson was looking at all of her records. Franklin's male research assistant was showing them to Watson in secret. Watson and Crick used Franklin's work to come up with the correct model. They never told Franklin, who died at an early age from cancer, what they had done. Franklin is recognized today for her vital role in the discovery of DNA's structure.

The True Story Behind DNA

Quiz

After reading the story, answer the questions.
Fill in the circle next to the correct answer.

1. This story is mainly about
   a) our genes and DNA.
   b) DNA's double helix.
   c) secretly looking at DNA data.
   d) the discovery of DNA's structure.

2. What year were Watson and Crick awarded the Nobel Prize?
   a) 1951
   b) 1952
   c) 1953
   d) 1954

3. Think about how the word *recognized* relates to *known*. Which words relate in the same way?

   | recognized : known |

   a) equal : unfair
   b) secret : known
   c) unusual : common
   d) vital : necessary

4. Which answer below is least likely to be an inherited characteristic?
   a) having long hair
   b) having curly hair
   c) having black hair
   d) having thick hair

5. From the story, one can tell that
   a) Franklin was not willing to help other researchers.
   b) Watson did not think Franklin's ideas were good enough to be shared.
   c) Franklin may have been given credit for her work earlier if she were a man.
   d) Franklin used Watson's data to prove that DNA's structure was a double helix.

New Words

Strange Stomach Stories

These are new words to practice.
Say each word 10 times.

* cylinders
* cords
* retrieved
* digestion

* gastric
* absorbed
* permanent
* acid

Before or after reading the story, write one sentence that contains at least one new word.

_____
_____
_____
_____

Strange Stomach Stories

René A.F. de Réaumur took small pieces of meat. He put the pieces in small metal cylinders. A cylinder is a round figure shaped like a can. The cylinders were filled with holes. Réaumur attached thin, strong cords to the cylinders. Then, he fed the meat-filled cylinders to hawks. After the hawks had gobbled down their meal and a certain amount of time had passed, Réaumur retrieved the cylinders from their stomachs by pulling on the cord.

Réaumur was a French scientist. The year was 1752. At that time, people knew very little about digestion. They did not know exactly how or where food was broken down and changed to a form that could be used by the body. Réaumur hoped to find out by examining the retrieved meat from the hawks' stomachs. Réaumur found that the meat had been partly digested by gastric juices, or chemicals, produced in the stomach. Réaumur showed that the stomach does more than grind up food. It produces chemicals to break it down.

Lazzaro Spallanzani, an Italian scientist, performed an experiment on himself in 1776. Spallanzani put a piece of a sponge in a small wire cage. After attaching a string to the cage, he swallowed it. Inside his stomach, the sponge absorbed, or soaked up, gastric juices. Spallanzani then pulled on the string and retrieved the sponge. He carefully squeezed the gastric juices the sponge had absorbed out. He mixed the retrieved juice with meat so he could observe what happened to the meat.

Lazzaro Spallanzani

In 1822, Alexis St. Martin, a French-Canadian fur trapper, was accidentally shot. He was left with a permanent hole in his stomach. The hole was 2 inches (5 cm) wide. Three years after the accident, William Beaumont, a U.S. Army surgeon, collected gastric juices produced in St. Martin's stomach through the permanent hole.

Beaumont found that the juices contained acid. The presence of acid proved that digestion is a chemical process carried out by chemicals in the stomach. Beaumont also observed what happened to different foods in the stomach. He found, for example, that vegetables were less digestible than other foods.

Strange Stomach Stories

Quiz

After reading the story, answer the questions.
Fill in the circle next to the correct answer.

1. Which answer is true?
   a) William Beaumont was shot.
   b) Spallanzani was an Italian scientist.
   c) René A.F. de Réaumur was French-Canadian.
   d) Alexis St. Martin was a U.S. Army surgeon.

2. This story is mainly about
   a) how food is digested.
   b) gastric juices in the stomach.
   c) meat-filled cylinders and feeding hawks.
   d) three scientists and how they studied digestion.

3. Why did Réaumur tie a cord onto the cylinders?
   a) to prove the stomach grinds food
   b) to retrieve the meat from the hawks' stomachs
   c) to observe what foods were the most digestible
   d) to collect the gastric juice absorbed by the sponge

4. Think about how the word *find* relates to *lose*. What words relate in the same way?

   find : lose

   a) observe : see
   b) produce : make
   c) retrieve : send
   d) examine : study

5. From the story, one can tell that
   a) no one studied digestion until 1752.
   b) St. Martin could only eat vegetables after being shot.
   c) U.S. scientists studied digestion more than anyone else.
   d) studying digestion was hard when one could not see inside the body.

#8037 Nonfiction Reading: Science ©Teacher Created Resources, Inc.

New Words

A Parachute and a Shark

**These are new words to practice.
Say each word 10 times.**

* naval
* deployed
* parachute
* vessel

* blubbery
* plankton
* coincidence
* transmitter

**Before or after reading the story, write one sentence
that contains at least one new word.**

_____

_____

_____

_____

A Parachute and a Shark

Story

A naval research ship was off the coast of the Hawaiian island of Oahu. On November 15, 1976, the navy crewmen deployed, or spread out, two parachutes. The parachutes were the vessel's sea anchors. One of the ship's anchors was deployed at about five hundred feet (152 meters) below the surface of the water. When the crew pulled the anchor up, they pulled up something else, too. They pulled up a shark that had swallowed the parachute!

No one on the naval vessel recognized the shark. No one knew what species, or kind, it was. No one had ever seen anything like it. It was over fourteen feet (four meters) long. It weighed 1,650 pounds (748 kilograms). It had enormous blubbery, or fat, lips that made it look like a seagoing hippopotamus. It had thousands of tiny teeth in its huge mouth.

The newly discovered species became known as the "megamouth." The megamouth is enormous. Why wasn't it discovered long ago? One reason might be because of what it eats. With its huge mouth and blubbery lips, the megamouth is a deepwater plankton feeder. Plankton are tiny animals that float in water. Because megamouths feed on plankton, it would be unlikely for one to ever take a baited hook.

The first megamouth was discovered because of a coincidence. A coincidence is a happening of events that seem to be connected, but the events are not connected. The megamouth was discovered because a ship deployed parachute anchors. The anchors were deployed where and when a megamouth was feeding. When one thinks about how big the ocean is and the timing, this is an amazing coincidence.

Only 32 other megamouths have been found since 1976. Some washed up on the shore. Others were trapped in nets. In 1990, one megamouth trapped off the California coast was fitted with a transmitter. The transmitter worked for two days. It told scientists that the shark spent the daytime hours in water between 400 and 550 feet (122 and 168 meters) deep. At night, it migrated up toward the surface.

megamouth

A Parachute and a Shark

Quiz

After reading the story, answer the questions.
Fill in the circle next to the correct answer.

1. A megamouth most likely would not be caught with a baited hook because it
   - (a) feeds on plankton.
   - (b) has thousands of tiny teeth.
   - (c) migrates up toward the surface at night.
   - (d) has a huge mouth and enormous blubbery lips.

2. The first megamouth was found off the coast of what island?
   - (a) Maui
   - (b) Oahu
   - (c) Kauai
   - (d) Hawaii

3. This story is mainly about
   - (a) scientific coincidences.
   - (b) sharks around the world.
   - (c) a discovery of a new species.
   - (d) fitting a megamouth with a transmitter.

4. Betty and Bart see each other at the movies. What would make it a coincidence?
   - (a) Betty wanted to surprise Bart.
   - (b) Betty and Bart planned to sit together.
   - (c) Betty had already seen the movie the day before.
   - (d) Betty and Bart did not know that the other was going.

5. Think about how the word *ship* relates to *vessel*. Which words relate in the same way?

   | ship : vessel |

   - (a) car : road
   - (b) oak : tree
   - (c) dog : puppy
   - (d) ocean : lake

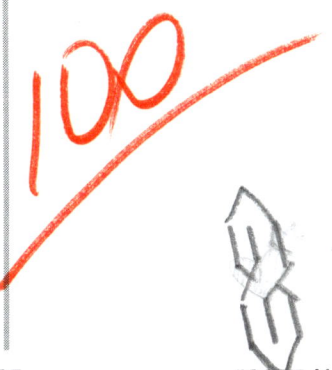

©Teacher Created Resources, Inc.

New Words

A True Case from 1856

These are new words to practice.

Say each word 10 times.

- sealed
- destination
- culprit
- official

- numerous
- university
- requested
- samples

Before or after reading the story, write one sentence that contains at least one new word.

_____

_____

_____

_____

A True Case from 1856

A barrel was filled with silver coins, sealed tightly, and placed on a train. Its destination was a station much further down the line. When the barrel reached its destination, it was still sealed. But when the barrel was opened, its precious contents were missing. The valuable coins were gone, and in their place was nothing but sand! Someone had opened the barrel and stolen the coins. Someone had resealed the barrel after refilling it with sand.

The theft occurred on a German train in 1856. No one believed the culprit, or guilty person, would ever be found. This was because no one knew about the robbery until the barrel had reached its destination. The train had made numerous stops along the way. The stops were all scheduled and at official stations along the track. The theft could have occurred at any one of the official station stops along the way.

The culprit was an employee who was sure that he would never be found out. This was because the train had made numerous stops. This was because at every stop the barrel looked like it held its original contents. The culprit thought he had been clever by refilling the barrel with sand and resealing it. He thought there was no way of knowing what station the theft had occurred at. It was an impossible case to solve!

A university professor in Berlin believed he could solve the case. The university professor requested, or asked, for samples of sand. He requested sand from every station that the train had stopped at when it was carrying the barrel. The professor examined the samples in his microscope. By examining the sand, he was able to match one of the samples to the sand in the barrel!

Once the professor told the police at which station the theft had occurred, the culprit was easily found, as there had only been a few employees on duty. People were astounded that the impossible case had been solved. We are used to scientific instruments helping solve crimes today, but 150 years ago, it was big news.

A True Case from 1856

Quiz

After reading the story, answer the questions.
Fill in the circle next to the correct answer.

1. This story is mainly about
   a) how a theft of silver coins occurred.
   b) why a professor requested sand samples.
   c) what a culprit did and how he was found out.
   d) using scientific instruments to solve crimes.

2. When something is sealed, it is
   a) found out.
   b) closed tightly.
   c) filled with sand.
   d) examined under a microscope.

3. Think about how the word *precious* relates to *valuable*. Which words relate in the same way?

   precious : valuable

   a) big : small
   b) empty : filled
   c) numerous : few
   d) astounding : surprising

4. The culprit thought he could never be found because he did not know that
   a) the sealed barrel would be opened when it was.
   b) there were just a few employees at every station.
   c) the sand he used was the same as the sand at other stations.
   d) there was a way to find out at which station the theft occurred.

5. From the story, one can tell that
   a) there is less crime because of scientific instruments.
   b) sometimes scientific instruments can help solve a crime.
   c) scientific instruments have always been used to solve crimes.
   d) no crime is impossible to solve with scientific instruments.

New Words

What Came First

**These are new words to practice.
Say each word 10 times.**

- topic
- query
- vitamin
- essential
- adequate
- stethoscope
- items
- extraordinary

Before or after reading the story, write one sentence that contains at least one new word.

_____

_____

_____

_____

What Came First

Today was "What Came First Day." The topic for this Friday's "What Came First Day" was inventions and discoveries. Mr. Cata said, "My query deals with the first color television system and the ballpoint pen. Which was invented first?" Juan answered Mr. Cata's query. He said that the ballpoint pen was invented first. It was invented in 1938. The color television system was invented later. It was invented in 1941.

Mr. Cata's next topic was about vitamins. Mr. Cata said, "Vitamin K is essential, or necessary, to blood clotting. Without an adequate, or sufficient, supply of vitamin K, our blood would take an abnormally long time to clot. Vitamin A is essential to skeletal growth. People without an adequate supply of vitamin A suffer from night blindness. Which vitamin was discovered first?" Lita answered. She knew that vitamin A was discovered in 1913. Vitamin K was discovered in 1934.

"My third query is on a medical topic," said Mr. Cata. "It is on medical instruments. Which was invented first: the stethoscope or the medical thermometer?" Mu Tan knew the answer. She knew that the medical thermometer was invented in 1616. The stethoscope was invented in 1816.

Mr. Cata queried, "What came first: DNA fingerprinting or the bar code system? Which invention came first?" Ken knew. He knew that the bar code system was first. It was invented in 1970. DNA fingerprinting was second. It was invented in 1986. Mr. Cata smiled. He told the class they were doing well.

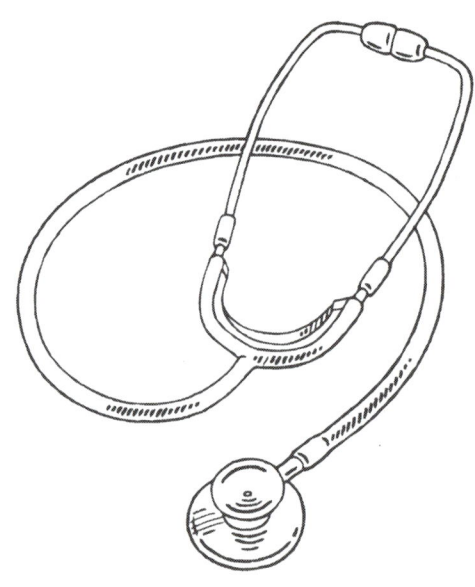

stethoscope

Mr. Cata said, "My last question is about two items. Today the items are common, but when they were first invented they were not ordinary. They were extraordinary. Which extraordinary item was invented first: the paper clip or the zipper?" The class thought hard. Amir knew. He told the class that the zipper was invented the same year as the flashlight, aluminum boat, and electric motor car. They were all invented in 1891. The paper clip was invented the same year as the tractor. It was invented in 1900. The zipper was first.

What Came First

Quiz

After reading the story, answer the questions. Fill in the circle next to the correct answer.

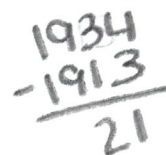

1. This story is mainly about
   a. who made the first inventions.
   b. what Mr. Cato's class invented.
   c. why "What Came First Day" was Friday.
   d. when inventions and discoveries took place.

2. Vitamin A was discovered about
   a. 21 years after vitamin K.
   b. 47 years after vitamin K.
   c. 21 years before vitamin K.
   d. 47 years before vitamin K.

3. Think about how the word *normal* relates to *abnormal*. Which words relate in the same way?

   normal : abnormal

   a. clotting : vitamin
   b. adequate : sufficient
   c. essential : necessary
   d. common : extraordinary

4. From the story, one can tell that the paper clip was invented after the
   a. tractor.
   b. bar code.
   c. stethoscope.
   d. ballpoint pen.

5. Which answer lists the items in the correct order of invention or discovery?
   a. zipper, vitamin K, bar code system
   b. stethoscope, vitamin A, electric motor car
   c. aluminum boat, medical thermometer, tractor
   d. DNA fingerprinting, paper clip, ballpoint pen

©Teacher Created Resources, Inc. 71 #8037 Nonfiction Reading: Science

The Most Expensive Rattle

**These are new words to practice.
Say each word 10 times.**

- aluminum
- element
- abundant
- compound
- isolated
- bauxite
- deposits
- alloys

Before or after reading the story, write one sentence that contains at least one new word.

_____
_____
_____
_____

The Most Expensive Rattle

In 1856 Napoleon III was the emperor of France. The emperor ordered a special rattle made. The rattle was for the emperor's son Prince Louis Napoleon. The rattle was very expensive. It was more expensive than a rattle made of pure gold. What was the rattle made of?

The rattle was made of the same material that soda pop cans are made of! The rattle was made of aluminum! Aluminum is an element. An element is a substance made up of only one type of atom. Aluminum is the most common metal in the world. It is the third-most abundant, or plentiful, element found on Earth. Only the elements silicon and oxygen are more abundant. The symbol for aluminum is Al.

When Napoleon ordered his son's rattle, aluminum was harder to obtain than gold. Its rareness created its value. Despite its abundance, aluminum, unlike gold, does not occur as a pure element in nature. It only occurs as a compound. A compound is a substance made of two or more elements. For aluminum to be used, it must first be isolated. It must be separated from other elements.

Bauxite is a compound found in nature that contains aluminum. Large deposits of bauxite are found in Australia, Brazil, Guinea, Jamaica, and Surinam. Bauxite deposits are mined in these countries. It is then heated and processed to isolate aluminum. During Napoleon's time, isolating aluminum was a new and costly process. Today, processing aluminum is much cheaper. It is mixed with other elements to form alloys. Aluminum alloys are light and strong. Aluminum and its alloys are used in cans. They are used in cars and planes. They are used in firefighters' flameproof suits.

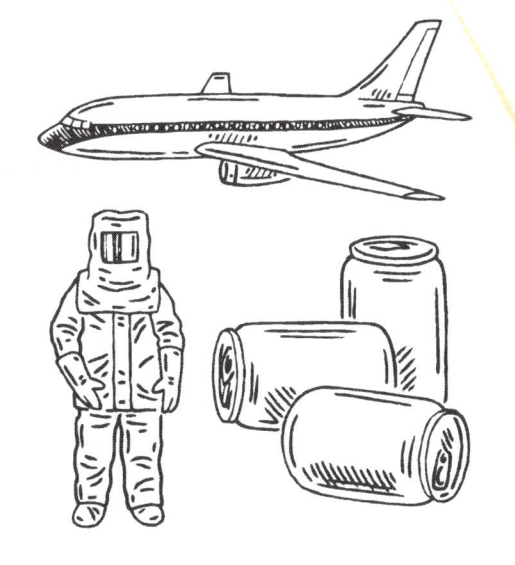

Aluminum is abundant, but it should be recycled. Why should it be recycled? It costs less energy and money to reuse aluminum than it does to mine and isolate it. Recycling means less bauxite needs to be mined. Four to five tons of bauxite is needed to produce about one ton of aluminum. Less mining means less of Earth's crust is cleared. More of the Earth is preserved.

The Most Expensive Rattle

Quiz

After reading the story, answer the questions.
Fill in the circle next to the correct answer.

1. This story is mainly about
   a. isolating aluminum.
   b. an abundant element.
   c. why aluminum was expensive.
   d. the rattle Napoleon ordered.

2. Which country is listed as having large deposits of bauxite?
   a. Brazil
   b. Guyana
   c. Jordan
   d. Austria

3. A proverb is a wise, old saying. What proverb best fits the last paragraph of this story?
   a. A rolling stone gathers no moss.
   b. Good fences make good neighbors.
   c. From little acorns mighty oaks do grow.
   d. A bird in the hand is worth two in the bush.

4. Gold is more expensive than aluminum today. Most likely, this is because
   a. gold is rarer.
   b. gold cannot be recycled.
   c. gold cannot be made into alloys.
   d. gold occurs as a pure element in nature.

5. Think about how the word *expensive* relates to *costly*. Which words relate in the same way?

   expensive : costly

   a. pure : mixed
   b. rare : common
   c. abundant : plentiful
   d. isolated : separated

New Words

The Mammal with a Suit of Armor

These are new words to practice.
Say each word 10 times.

- bony
- armor
- quadruplets
- leprosy

- traits
- armadillo
- litter
- saliva

Before or after reading the story, write one sentence that contains at least one new word.

_____
_____
_____
_____

The Mammal with a Suit of Armor

All mammals are warm-blooded animals. All mammals have backbones. All mammals have hair. All female mammals have glands that produce milk for feeding their young. Only one mammal has a suit of bony armor. Only one mammal's pups, or young, are identical quadruplets. Only one mammal besides humans can be infected with leprosy. What mammal has these three special traits, or characteristics?

The armadillo is the mammal with these special traits. There are 20 different kinds of armadillos. The smallest one is the fairy armadillo. From head to tail, it measures about 6–7 inches (15–18 cm). It weighs just 3 ounces (85 gm). The largest one is the giant armadillo. It measures 48–59 inches (122–150 cm) from head to tail. It weighs 100–132 pounds (45–60 kgs). Armadillos are found in southern North America, Central America, and South America.

An armadillo's armor is made up of bony bands, or strips. Its skin is stretched over the bony plates. The skin is covered in hard, tough scales. The scales are made up of the same material that makes up one's fingernails and the horns of a cow. Its hair is sparse, or thinly spread.

armadillo

A litter is all the pups or young born to an animal at one time. Armadillo litters are either all boys or all girls. This is because females always give birth to identical quadruplets. All four babies come from a single egg. Armadillos have long, strong tongues covered with sticky saliva. The sticky saliva helps armadillos trap insects by "gluing" them to its tongue. A giant armadillo can stick its tongue into an insect nest and collect as many as 40,000 ants or termites on its tongue at one time!

Leprosy, also known as Hansen's Disease, is a horrible disease. It is caused by a germ, or kind of bacteria. It attacks the skin and nerves. In severe cases, people have lost ears, fingers, toes, and the ends of other body parts. Armadillos have been very helpful to doctors trying to find a cure of leprosy. This is because armadillos are the only animals in the world besides humans that can fall victim to leprosy.

The Mammal with a Suit of Armor

Quiz

After reading the story, answer the questions.
Fill in the circle next to the correct answer.

1. What helps an armadillo trap insects?

- a) its armor
- b) its tail
- c) its litter
- **d) its saliva**

2. One reason some armadillos may be able to protect themselves by rolling into a ball is because they are covered with

- a) sparse hair rather than thick hair.
- b) hard, scaly skin rather than soft skin.
- **c) bony bands rather than one solid bone plate.**
- d) the material that makes up fingernails rather than horns.

3. This story is mainly about

- **a) one mammal's traits.**
- b) all warm-blooded mammals.
- c) the suit of armor of one mammal.
- d) one mammal helping to cure a terrible disease.

4. If a girl baby armadillo is born, it

- a) will be identical to its mother.
- **b) will have three identical sisters.**
- c) will have three sisters or brothers.
- d) will have come from a different egg than its sisters.

5. Think about how the word *quadruplets* relates to *four*. Which words relate in the same way?

| quadruplets : four |

- a) twins : six
- b) triplets : two
- **c) quintuplets : five**
- d) sextuplets : three

100

New Words

Moon Rocks

**These are new words to practice.
Say each word 10 times.**

- task
- lunar
- sole
- retrieved
- quarantined
- chambers
- microorganisms
- monitored

Before or after reading the story, write one sentence that contains at least one new word.

_____
_____
_____
_____

Moon Rocks

On July 20, 1969, Neil Armstrong became the first man to walk on the moon. His first and most immediate task was to collect lunar soil. Lunar soil consists of rock and dust. Armstrong immediately scooped up about two pounds (.9 kg) of lunar soil. After he bagged the soil, he carefully placed it in a pocket on the thigh of his spacesuit. The pocket's sole, or only, purpose was to hold the lunar soil.

Why was Armstrong's first and most immediate task to collect lunar soil? Why was there a pocket built solely to hold it? No one knew what would happen when Armstrong stepped onto the moon. If the mission had to be aborted, or stopped abruptly, then at least the astronauts would not return to Earth empty-handed.

A total of 843 pounds (380 kg) of lunar soil has been brought to Earth over the years. When the soil was first retrieved, or carried back, it was quarantined. When something is quarantined, it is kept in isolation. It is kept apart. The rocks were kept in airtight chambers, or rooms. Scientists outside the chambers handled the rocks. They handled the rocks with gloves sealed into openings in the chamber walls.

The retrieved rocks were quarantined because scientists did not know if they carried microorganisms or other tiny life forms on or in them. They did not know if these microorganisms or other life forms could harm us. The rocks are no longer quarantined now that scientists know that the rocks are safe, but they are still carefully monitored, or watched.

The rocks are carefully monitored because there is a limited supply and so they are very valuable. They are worth up to 10 times their weight in top-grade diamonds. Most of the rocks are stored in government strongholds, but some are lent to researchers, museums, and even schools. Some of the rocks were given away. Tiny pebbles were given to 135 nations and each of the 50 states. Sometimes rocks are stolen, but if a thief is caught selling one, he or she is punished severely.

Moon Rocks

Quiz

After reading the story, answer the questions.
Fill in the circle next to the correct answer.

1. One reason there is a limited supply of moon rocks is that
   a. some of the rocks are stolen.
   b. they are quarantined for safety reasons.
   c. only a certain number of rocks were retrieved.
   d. some of the rocks were given away to other nations.

2. This story is mainly about
   a. retrieved lunar soil.
   b. monitored lunar soil.
   c. quarantined lunar soil.
   d. Neil Armstrong's lunar soil.

3. Where did Armstrong put the lunar soil he first collected?
   a. in a back pocket of his spacesuit
   b. in a pocket on the thigh of his spacesuit
   c. in a pocket on the sleeve of his spacesuit
   d. in a pocket on the chest of his spacesuit

4. Think about how the word *chamber* relates to *room*. Which words relate in the same way?

   chamber : room

   a. task : job
   b. moon : earth
   c. pebble : diamond
   d. thief : astronaut

5. What was the total number of gift rocks mentioned in the story?
   a. 85
   b. 185
   c. 285
   d. 385

#8037 Nonfiction Reading: Science 80 ©Teacher Created Resources, Inc.

New Words

Injecting Poison on Purpose

These are new words to practice.

Say each word 10 times.

- botulism
- toxin
- fatal
- inject

- spores
- contaminate
- antitoxins
- paralyzed

Before or after reading the story, write one sentence that contains at least one new word.

_____
_____
_____
_____

Injecting Poison on Purpose

Story

Botulism is a form of food poisoning. Botulism is caused by a toxin, or poison. The toxin is made by bacteria. The bacteria are called *Clostridium botulinum*. Severe cases of botulism are often fatal, or deadly. It would seem that people would want nothing to do with this toxin. Yet doctors use this highly poisonous toxin. Doctors purposefully inject it into their patients. What is going on?

Botulism-causing bacteria lives in the soil. In the soil, the bacteria produce spores. The spores have only one cell. They are heat-resistant. They will produce bacteria under the right conditions. Sometimes the spores will contaminate fresh food used for canning. If the contaminated food is not heated up to a high temperature for a certain length of time, the heat-resistant spores will survive inside the can. Bacteria will multiply. Inside the can, the bacteria will release its deadly toxin.

It is important to properly heat canned food before eating it. This is because heat will destroy any toxin released by bacteria inside the can. If the toxin is not destroyed, one can become fatally ill. The person may die if antitoxins are not given in time. Antitoxins work against the toxins.

If one is poisoned, one will first suffer from nausea and vomiting. Then one will feel tired. One's head may ache, and one may feel dizzy. One may have difficulty seeing. One may begin to have difficulty swallowing and speaking. The muscles one uses to breathe may become paralyzed. Doctors know this toxin can be deadly if eaten. They know it can stop muscle movement and cause paralysis. Yet they use it for this very reason.

Doctors use the toxin to treat patients who suffer from uncontrollable twitching. To treat the patient, the doctor injects a tiny amount of toxin into the twitching muscles. When the toxin is injected, it blocks the messages going from the nerves to the muscles. The muscles become paralyzed. They stop twitching. Sometimes, doctors inject this toxin into patients' face muscles. Paralyzing the muscles smoothes out wrinkles. The effects of the injection usually last only a few months.

Quiz

Injecting Poison on Purpose

**After reading the story, answer the questions.
Fill in the circle next to the correct answer.**

1. One should always properly heat food eaten from a can so that
   - (a) toxins are destroyed.
   - (b) antitoxins are injected.
   - (c) bacteria are contaminated.
   - (d) heat-resistant spores are killed.

2. This story is mainly about
   - (a) doctors.
   - (b) a toxin.
   - (c) bacteria.
   - (d) food poisoning.

3. What is not listed as a symptom of botulism poisoning?
   - (a) nausea
   - (b) a headache
   - (c) feeling hot
   - (d) difficulty speaking

4. Think about how the word *fatal* relates to *deadly*. Which words relate in the same way?

   fatal : deadly

   - (a) toxic : poisonous
   - (b) contaminated : clean
   - (c) injected : swallowed
   - (d) twitching : paralyzed

5. Doctors use the toxin because it
   - (a) is destroyed with heat.
   - (b) can be injected with antitoxins.
   - (c) paralyzes muscles one uses to breathe.
   - (d) blocks messages going from nerves to muscles.

The 5,000-Year-Old Man

**These are new words to practice.
Say each word 10 times.**

- encased
- assumed
- authorities
- retain
- preserved
- archaeologists
- artifacts
- embers

Before or after reading the story, write one sentence that contains at least one new word.

_____
_____
_____
_____

The 5,000-Year-Old Man

Helmut and Erika Simon were hiking. They were high in the Italian Alps. The date was September 19, 1991. Spotting something brown in the ice, they walked over to investigate. They found a body facing downward. The scalp, shoulders, and back were free from the ice. The rest of the body was still encased, or covered completely, in the ice. The Simons assumed, or believed, it was a hiker that had been recently lost, and they reported their find to the authorities.

The authorities checked their records. They assumed it was a hiker lost in 1938. Most likely, he had gotten lost during a storm. Encased in ice, he had just now been pushed down and out by the glacier. What the authorities found was a mummy more than 5,000 years old. Mummies are more than skeletons. They retain, or keep, body tissues. The body had dried out and then been preserved, or kept from rotting, under layers of ice.

Archaeologists are scientists who study ancient times and people. Archaeologists study artifacts, or things made by human work or skill, to help them learn about the past. By examining the mummy and the preserved artifacts on his person and around him, archaeologists were able to learn much about what we call the Neolithic time period.

Among the artifacts the archaeologists studied were two fire kits. The first kit was a birch bark container. It was used to carry glowing embers, or tiny burning bits of charcoal. Fresh maple leaves, still retaining a bit of their green color, lined the container. The lining was to prevent the embers from causing the container to catch on fire.

The second kit was a back-up kit. It contained the middle part of a fungus. The fungus lives on dead or diseased beech trees. The middle part of the fungus, and only the middle part, is very useful in starting fires. Scientists studied the fungus with an electron microscope. They found tiny particles in it. The particles came from pyrites, a useful material in starting fires made of sulfur and iron.

The 5,000-Year-Old Man

Quiz

After reading the story, answer the questions. Fill in the circle next to the correct answer.

1. Which part of the mummy was not encased in ice?
   - (a) face
   - (b) hands
   - (c) scalp ●
   - (d) stomach

2. This story is mainly about
   - (a) a mummy and artifacts. ●
   - (b) what archaeologists found.
   - (c) two hikers in the Italian Alps.
   - (d) a fire-starting kit and a back-up kit.

3. Normally, a body frozen in a glacier would be ground to bits as the glacier moved. One reason the mummy's body did not break up might be that it was
   - (a) covered in tiny iron particles.
   - (b) in the middle, preserved by a fungus.
   - (c) discovered soon after it was encased in ice.
   - (d) in a hollow, and the glacier flowed over its top. ●

4. Think about how the word *preserve* relates to *spoil*. Which words relate in the same way?

   preserve : spoil

   - (a) hike : walk
   - (b) retain : lose ●
   - (c) study : examine
   - (d) encase : surround

5. From the story, one can tell that how to make a fire was discovered
   - (a) after the Neolithic period.
   - (b) during the Neolithic period.
   - (c) before the Neolithic period.
   - (d) in or before the Neolithic period. ●

A Quiver of Cobras

**These are new words to practice.
Say each word 10 times.**

- threatened
- expand
- venom
- neurotoxin
- inject
- nocturnal
- diurnal
- juvenile

Before or after reading the story, write one sentence that contains at least one new word.

_____
_____
_____
_____

A Quiver of Cobras

A person wearing sunglasses nears a spitting cobra. The snake feels threatened, or in possible danger. To look bigger and make it appear more threatening, the cobra raises its head. It expands its hood. To expand, or flare, the hood, the cobra spreads a series of small ribs outward with its neck muscles. The cobra waves back and forth, but the person continues to approach.

When the person is seven feet (2.1 m) away, the cobra pulls its head back and then whips it forward. At the same time that it whips its head forward, the cobra spits, releasing venom from its fangs. The venom is a deadly neurotoxin. A neurotoxin is a poison that attacks the nervous system. The venom is so deadly that less than 0.035 ounces (one gram) is enough to kill 50 adult humans. The person is sprayed with venom on the face, but the person is unhurt. How could this be?

The person's sunglasses acted as a shield. The sunglasses protected the person's eyes from the venom. If the venom had entered the person's eyes or an open wound, the person would have been blinded and in great pain. The kinds of cobras that spit venom are protecting themselves, not hunting. When hunting, all cobras bite and inject poison into their victims. A cobra can inject enough poison in a single bite to kill an elephant.

A group of cobras is called a quiver. These venomous reptiles belong to the *Elapidae* family, along with other venomous snakes such as coral snakes, kraits, sea snakes, and mambas. Most cobras are nocturnal. A nocturnal animal is one that is active mostly at night.

Adult red spitting cobras are nocturnal, but juvenile, or young cobras, are diurnal. A diurnal animal is one that is active mostly during the day. Scientists think one reason adult red spitting cobras are nocturnal and juveniles are diurnal is that this type of cobra is cannibalistic. The adult snakes will eat their young.

A Quiver of Cobras

Quiz

After reading the story, answer the questions.
Fill in the circle next to the correct answer.

1. This story is mainly about
   a. venom.
   b. **cobras.**
   c. snakes.
   d. reptiles.

2. What snake is not a member of the *Elapidae* family?
   a. krait
   b. mamba
   c. **python**
   d. sea snake

3. Think about how the word *quiver* relates to *cobra*. Which words relate in the same way?

   > quiver : cobra

   a. **pack : wolf**
   b. horse : herd
   c. sheep : flock
   d. gosling : goose

4. Choose the word that best completes this sentence: "When a cobra spits, it feels _threatened_."
   a. hooded.
   b. blinded.
   c. protected.
   d. **threatened.**

5. Which statement is true?
   a. All cobras spit.
   b. All reptiles are venomous.
   c. All diurnal snakes are juveniles.
   d. **All nocturnal snakes are active mostly at night.**

The Price of a Crooked Finger

New Words

**These are new words to practice.
Say each word 10 times.**

- dislocated
- athletic
- participate
- bloomers
- conformity
- bacteriologist
- advocated
- pasteurize

Before or after reading the story, write one sentence that contains at least one new word.

_____
_____
_____
_____

The Price of a Crooked Finger

Alice Evans went to the doctor. She had dislocated her finger. The doctor refused to set Evans's finger back in place! The doctor should have and could have set the finger, but he would not. Instead, the doctor said Evans had to suffer the result of her actions. What was Evans doing that caused her finger to become dislocated? What was she doing that was so bad that she should have to suffer the results of her actions?

Evans dislocated her finger while playing basketball. Evans was born in 1881. When Evans was 18, she played on a newly organized college basketball team. At that time, women were not encouraged to be athletic. Women were not supposed to sweat. Women who participated in athletics were considered unladylike.

To participate, Evans and her teammates had to dress a special way. They covered their bodies in black. They wore heavy knit sweaters that covered their arms and necks. They wore baggy, woolen bloomers. Bloomers were full, loose trousers that were gathered at the bottom. They wore leather high-topped shoes. They wore long, thick stockings.

Alice Evans

Evans's finger healed over time, but because it was not set, it remained slightly out of joint for the rest of her life. In her memoirs or autobiography, Evans said that her finger was "a reminder that if someone oversteps conformity, one is apt to have to pay a price." When one conforms, one acts or behaves the way one is required to. Evans' price for not conforming and behaving "unladylike" was a crooked finger.

Despite social objections, Evans became a bacteriologist. At the time, there were very few female scientists or bacteriologists. Evans discovered bacteria in raw milk could cause people to become deathly ill. She advocated, or supported, laws that required raw milk to be pasteurized. When something is pasteurized, it is heated up to a certain temperature for a certain amount of time. The process kills harmful bacteria. Raw milk began to be pasteurized in the 1930s. Thanks to Evans' scientific work and advocacy, countless lives have been saved.

The Price of a Crooked Finger

Quiz

After reading the story, answer the questions.
Fill in the circle next to the correct answer.

1. What was not part of Evans's basketball uniform?
   - a) heavy knit sweaters
   - b) short, thick stockings
   - c) loose, woolen bloomers
   - d) high-topped leather shoes

2. Why did Evans advocate that raw milk should be pasteurized?
   - a) She knew there was a price to be paid for not conforming.
   - b) She discovered harmful bacteria in it that could be killed by heat.
   - c) She knew that more women would participate in pasteurization than athletics.
   - d) She wanted to stop people from getting deathly ill because the doctor might not treat them.

3. This story is mainly about
   - a) women's athletics long ago.
   - b) why milk is pasteurized today.
   - c) a bacteriologist born in 1881.
   - d) if a doctor should have set a finger.

4. From the story, one can tell that Evans most likely
   - a) hated the way her finger looked.
   - b) thought the doctor was right to make her suffer.
   - c) would have liked someone else to write her memoirs.
   - d) was more interested in doing what interested her than conforming.

5. Think about how the word *advocate* relates to *support*. Which words relate in the same way?

   advocate : support

   - a) cover : hide
   - b) refuse : allow
   - c) remain : change
   - d) participate : quit

May I Draw a Round Perimeter?

New Words

These are new words to practice.
Say each word 10 times.

- pi
- ratio
- diameter
- circumference
- perimeter
- approximated
- digits
- mnemonic

Before or after reading the story, write one sentence that contains at least one new word.

_____
_____
_____
_____

May I Draw a Round Perimeter?

Pi is a very special number. Pi is a ratio. A ratio is a comparison of two numbers by division. A circle's diameter is a line segment. The line segment has its endpoints on the circle. The line segment contains the center of the circle. The circumference of a circle is its perimeter, or distance around. Pi is the ratio of the circumference of any circle to the length of its diameter.

Take any circle and divide its circumference by its diameter. The answer is always the same. It is always pi. The symbol for pi is π. Pi can only be approximated. An approximation is not exact. People have to approximate pi because the diameter never divides into the circumference evenly. It has an endless number of digits. 3.14 and 22/7 are approximations of pi.

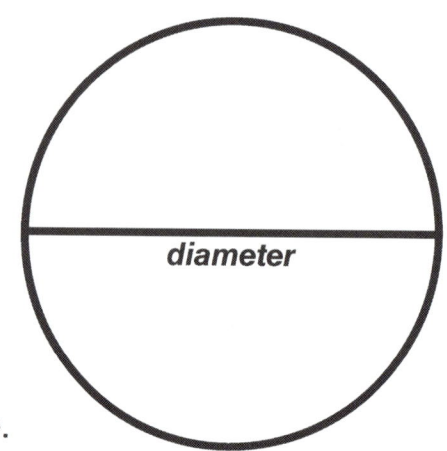

"May I draw a round perimeter" is a mnemonic phrase. A mnemonic has to do with memory. A mnemonic phrase helps one to remember. The first six digits of pi are 3.14159. "May I draw a round perimeter" helps one remember these digits because of the number of letters in each word. The word "may" has three letters. The word "I" has one letter. The word "draw" has four letters. The words "a," "round," and "perimeter," have one, five, and nine letters. The numbers of letters in each word match the numbers 3.14159.

How many digits of pi are there? No one knows. In 2002, a supercomputer was programmed to figure it out. The computer went to 1.24 trillion decimal places before it was stopped! Pi, it seems, is a number without a pattern that never ends.

Contests are held to see who can memorize the most digits of pi. Akira Haraguchi set the current record in October 2006. To set the record, Haraguchi recited digits for sixteen hours. He took short five-minute breaks every hour or two to eat rice balls and use the restroom. He was monitored and videotaped the entire time. How many digits did Haraguchi recite? He recited pi to 100,000 decimal places!

The First 50 Digits of Pi

3.14159265358979323846264338327950288419716939937510

May I Draw a Round Perimeter?

Quiz

After reading the story, answer the questions.
Fill in the circle next to the correct answer.

1. This story is mainly about
   - a) a contest.
   - **b) a special ratio.**
   - c) an approximation.
   - d) a mnemonic phrase.

2. The supercomputer figured out pi to how many decimal places?
   - a) 1,240
   - b) 1,240,000
   - c) 1,240,000,000
   - **d) 1,240,000,000,000**

3. The names of the Great Lakes are Huron, Ontario, Michigan, Erie, and Superior. Tess used the mnemonic HOMES to help remember the names. How does this mnemonic work?
   - a) It matches a ratio to each lake name.
   - **b) It contains the first letter of each lake name.**
   - c) It uses great big capitals like the Great Lakes.
   - d) It makes one think of what state each lake is home to.

4. Why was Haraguchi monitored and videotaped even when he took a short break?
   - **a) to show that he did not cheat**
   - b) to record the number of hours
   - c) to keep his time from being approximated
   - d) to match his numbers with the supercomputer's

5. Think about how the word *recite* relates to *say*. Which words relate in the same way?

   recite : say

   - a) set : record
   - b) divide : count
   - c) approximate : match
   - **d) memorize : remember**

Why Warm Flowers?

New Words

These are new words to practice.
Say each word 10 times.

- botany
- botanist
- regulates
- advantage
- thrive
- pollination
- pistil
- stamen

Before or after reading the story, write one sentence that contains at least one new word.

_____
_____
_____
_____

Why Warm Flowers?

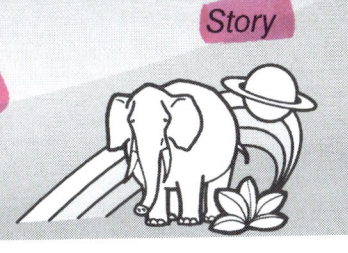

Botany is the study of plants and how they grow. A scientist who studies botany is called a botanist. Botanists have recently discovered an amazing thing about an Australian plant. The plant is called the sacred lotus. Botanists have discovered that the plant regulates, or controls, the temperature of its flowers! It keeps its flowers warm!

Why would a plant regulate temperature? What advantages could come from regulating flower temperature? Botanists have come up with two reasons why the lotus may thrive, or do well, with warm flowers. The first advantage has to do with flower development. Flowers may develop faster at warmer temperatures. The sooner a plant has flowers, the sooner it can begin to make seeds.

The second advantage has to do with pollination. Pollination must take place for a plant to make seeds. For pollination to occur, pollen must get to a plant's pistil. Pollen is a powdery substance produced in a plant's stamen. The pistil is the plant's egg-bearing organ. The stamen and pistil are flower parts. Different plants are pollinated in different ways. Some plants are self-pollinators. They pollinate themselves. Pollen drops from the plant's stamens into its pistils.

Other plants are cross-pollinators. In cross-pollination, pollen from one plant is transferred to another plant. Tiny pollen grains stick to the heads or bodies of pollinators such as bats, insects, or birds when they feed from or touch a flower. When the pollinator moves on, it transfers the pollen to another flower. The sacred lotus is cross-pollinated. Often, the pollinator is a beetle that is not active when it is cold.

Lotus plants close their petals in the evening. When the petals close, they trap the beetles inside. The beetles remain active because of the flower's warmth. As the beetle moves around inside the flower, its body becomes covered in pollen. A pollen-covered beetle helps the plant thrive. This is because in the morning the lotus plant will open its petals. The beetle will fly to other flowers. Pollen from the lotus will fall off the beetle and drop onto every flower that it visits.

lotus plant

Why Warm Flowers? — Quiz

After reading the story, answer the questions. Fill in the circle next to the correct answer.

1. What is the name of the plant's egg-bearing organ?
   a) seed
   b) pistil ●
   c) stamen
   d) pollen

2. This story is mainly about
   a) the field of botany.
   b) what some botanists discovered.
   c) pollination and how plants make seeds.
   d) why one plant may regulate temperature. ●

3. If the sacred lotus plant's flowers were as cold as the night air,
   a) the beetles would not be as active. ●
   b) the plant would be a self-pollinator.
   c) the pollen would not stick to the beetle.
   d) the flower would be pollinated in a different way.

4. Think about how the word *discover* relates to *find*. Which words relate in the same way?

   discover : find

   a) begin : end
   b) move : stay
   c) close : open
   d) thrive : grow ●

5. Plants that develop advantages when it comes to pollination may be able to grow more plants because they
   a) can regulate pollen.
   b) can close its petals.
   c) can produce more seeds. ●
   d) can use more than one kind of pollinator.

Space Animals

New Words

**These are new words to practice.
Say each word 10 times.**

- breed
- mongrel
- extensive
- acceleration
- gravity
- adapt
- osteoporosis
- includes

Before or after reading the story, write one sentence that contains at least one new word.

_____

_____

_____

_____

Space Animals

Story

The first living thing to be shot into space and orbit the planet was a dog. The dog's name was Laika. "Laika" means "little lemon." Laika was not a special breed of dog. She was a mongrel, or mix of several breeds. Laika may have been just a mongrel, but she made history when she flew on the Russian spacecraft *Sputnik 2* in 1957.

Laika

Before her flight, Laika underwent extensive training. When something is extensive, it is far-reaching. It applies to many things. Laika's extensive training included getting used to small spaces and loud noises. It included getting used to high acceleration forces. Laika had to learn not to panic when she felt the spacecraft accelerate, or speed up, quickly.

The next two animals shot into space were dogs, too. The dogs went up in Sputnik 5, a year after Laika. One of the dogs gave birth to a litter of six puppies after her return. John F. Kennedy, the president of the United States, received one of the puppies as a gift. Kennedy helped to launch the American space program. The first animals Americans sent into space were monkeys and chimpanzees. The animals were used to test the effects of high acceleration and equipment for manned spaceflights.

Today, human astronauts pilot missions. Still, animals are an important part of the space program. Scientists use animals for experiments. The experiments are designed to help scientists learn about the effects of living in zero gravity. They are designed to help learn more about how animals can adapt, or change. For example, astronauts brought spiders on a 1973 space mission. At first, the spiders could not build webs in the zero gravity. As the spiders adapted to zero gravity, their skills returned.

Osteoporosis is a weakening of the bones. People on Earth suffer from osteoporosis. Astronauts in zero gravity suffer from it, too. Rats and mice are part of space experiments designed to help scientists learn more about osteoporosis. The list of animals sent into space includes moths and flies. It includes frogs and newts. It includes minnows and goldfish.

Space Animals

Quiz

After reading the story, answer the questions. Fill in the circle next to the correct answer.

1. This story is mainly about
   - (a) some animal experiments.
   - (b) how animals adapt in space.
   - (c) Laika, the first animal in space.
   - ● animals that have been sent into space.

2. How many puppies were in the space dog's litter?
   - (a) 2
   - (b) 4
   - ● 6
   - (d) 8

3. Think about how the word *adapts* relates to *changes*. Which words relate in the same way?

   | adapts : changes |

   - (a) includes : cuts out
   - (b) receives : tests on
   - ● launches : starts up
   - (d) accelerates : slows down

4. Why might animals have been sent into space before people?
   - ● Scientists wanted to test equipment.
   - (b) Scientists needed time to design experiments.
   - (c) Animals were better at undergoing extensive training.
   - (d) Animals are not affected by high acceleration forces.

5. What stands out about the list of animals sent into space on manned spaceflights?
   - ● They are all small.
   - (b) They are all mammals.
   - (c) They are all able to swim.
   - (d) They are all suffering from osteoporosis.

100

"Operation Successful, Patient Died"

New Words

These are new words to practice.
Say each word 10 times.

- entry
- surgeon
- gangrene
- decay
- amputate
- limbs
- post-operation
- antiseptic

Before or after reading the story, write one sentence that contains at least one new word.

_____
_____
_____
_____

"Operation Successful, Patient Died"

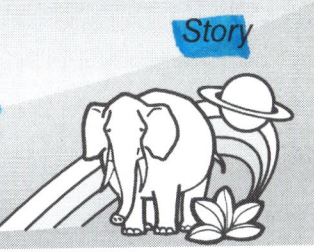

"Operation successful, patient died" was a common entry in 19th century medical records. The entry does not seem to make sense. It would seem that if an operation were successful, a patient would not die. A patient would survive. Yet in many hospitals, over half of the patients who were "successfully" operated on died. They died after the surgery. They died from infection. Doctors did not know why this was happening. The problem was called "hospitalism."

Joseph Lister was born in England in 1827. He went to medical school and became a surgeon. Many of Lister's patients suffered from gangrene. Gangrene occurs when the blood supply to part of the body is stopped. Body tissue or flesh begins to decay, or rot. During Lister's time, the common practice was to amputate, or cut off, gangrenous body parts. The most common body parts to develop gangrene were arms and legs.

Joseph Lister

Lister was a skilled surgeon. He performed many successful amputations in which he removed his patients' limbs. Despite Lister's skill and care, his patients became ill after surgery. His patients died from post-operation infections. Lister was determined to find out why patients still developed gangrene after otherwise successful operations. He wanted to decrease the number of entries that said, "Operation successful, patient died." He wanted to stop "hospitalism."

Lister read a series of articles written by Louis Pasteur. Pasteur's paper introduced the idea of disease-causing germs. Lister wondered if germs were the cause of his patient's post-operation infections. To find out, Lister changed the way he operated. He sought out ways to ensure that the patient remained germ-free after removal of decaying limbs.

More and more of Lister's patients began to recover. Lives were saved as Lister's practices were copied. Cases of "hospitalism" went down. What did Lister do? He washed his hands. He made hospitals change the sheets between patients. He made doctors wear clean coats. He made doctors clean their surgical instruments. He wiped everything down with an antiseptic. An antiseptic is a chemical substance that kills germs.

"Operation Successful, Patient Died"

Quiz

After reading the story, answer the questions.
Fill in the circle next to the correct answer.

1. This story is mainly about
   - (a) a surgeon who wrote about germs.
   - (b) a surgeon who developed gangrene.
   - (c) a surgeon who made medical record entries.
   - (d) a surgeon who decreased patient infections.

2. Gangrene occurs when the blood supply to part of the body is
   - (a) stopped.
   - (b) decayed.
   - (c) infected.
   - (d) amputated.

3. From the story, one can tell that
   - (a) successful amputations have decreased.
   - (b) medical entries today list antiseptics.
   - (c) Pasteur wrote about "hospitalism" in his articles.
   - (d) Lister's practices helped stop the spread of germs.

4. What is not listed as one of Lister's practices?
   - (a) wearing a mask
   - (b) using an antiseptic
   - (c) changing bed sheets
   - (d) cleaning surgical instruments

5. Think about how the word *surgeon* relates to *doctor*. Which words relate in the same way?

   | surgeon : doctor |

   - (a) body : rot
   - (b) leg : limb
   - (c) patient : hospital
   - (d) infection : operation

#8037 Nonfiction Reading: Science   104   ©Teacher Created Resources, Inc.

New Words

The Missing Crust

**These are new words to practice.
Say each word 10 times.**

- crust
- variable
- basin
- mantle
- vast
- exposed
- opportunity
- device

Before or after reading the story, write one sentence that contains at least one new word.

The Missing Crust

The crust is Earth's hard outer shell. Our continents and ocean basins are all part of the crust. The crust is the thinnest of Earth's four layers. The layers, from surface to center, are crust, mantle, outer core, and inner core.

The crust has a variable thickness. When something is variable, it is not the same. It changes. Through the continents, the crust is 21–42 miles (35–70 km) thick. It is 3–6 miles (5–10 km) thick through the ocean basins.

Scientists have recently found a vast, or huge, hole in the Earth's crust. The vast hole is about 3 miles (5 km) below the surface of the Atlantic Ocean. Scientists are very excited about this discovery. This is because in the absence of the crust, the mantle is exposed, or uncovered.

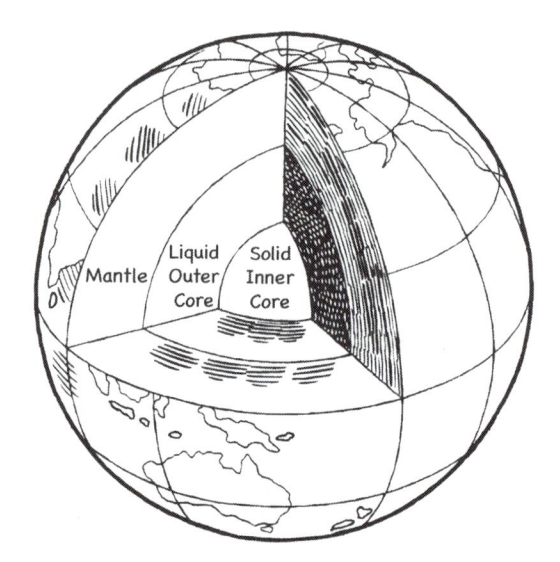

The exposed rock of the mantle provides scientists with an opportunity of study. Scientists will use a robotic device to help them study the mantle. The robotic device—named "Toby"—will be lowered from a research ship, where it will dive down to the exposed mantle. There, Toby will drill into the rock and collect samples. It will take pictures, too.

Why is part of the crust missing? Scientists do not have a complete explanation. Scientists know that the crust is divided into huge slabs called plates. The plates float on molten, or melted, rock. The floating plates drift very slowly, some drifting apart, and others crashing into each other. Scientists know that the mantle is exposed at an area that is part of a globe-spanning ridge of undersea volcanoes. It is exposed at a place where the plates drifted apart.

Usually volcanic lava would surge up to fill in the gap where the plates drifted apart. Scientists do not yet know why the gap has not filled with lava. They cannot explain why instead of crust there is a 30-mile (48 km) stretch of dark, green rock that makes up the deep inner layer of the Earth. What scientists do know is that the missing crust provides a rare opportunity to study the inner Earth.

The Missing Crust

After reading the story, answer the questions. Fill in the circle next to the correct answer.

1. The missing crust is below the surface of which ocean?
   - (a) Arctic
   - (b) Indian
   - (c) Pacific
   - ● Atlantic

2. Which question is not answered by the story?
   - (a) Which layer of the Earth is thinnest?
   - ● How was the hole in the crust found?
   - (c) What is Earth's innermost layer called?
   - (d) How will mantle rock samples be collected?

3. This story is mainly about
   - ● a hole in Earth's crust.
   - (b) Earth's deep inner mantle.
   - (c) how Toby will help scientists.
   - (d) the layers Earth is divided into.

4. From the story, one can tell that the plates are moving because
   - (a) they are huge slabs.
   - (b) they have missing parts.
   - (c) they divide up the crust.
   - ● they are floating on molten rock.

5. Think about how the word *cup* relates to *glass*. Which words relate in the same way?

   | cup : glass |

   - (a) knife : cut
   - (b) fork : spoon
   - ● bowl : basin
   - (d) chair : table

New Words

The Abandoned City of the Future

These are new words to practice.
Say each word 10 times.

- evacuated
- residents
- abandoned
- fission
- nucleus
- radioactive
- decay
- radiation

Before or after reading the story, write one sentence that contains at least one new word.

_____

_____

_____

_____

The Abandoned City of the Future

49,000 thousand people were told, "Tomorrow you will be evacuated. You will be taken away. Everyone must leave. Bring only what you will need for three days. There has been an accident." The people were residents of Pripyat. Pripyat is a city in Ukraine. Ukraine is known for its flat, fertile plains called steppes. Ukraine is located in southeastern Europe. It was part of the Soviet Union until independence was declared in 1991.

2,000 buses lined up to carry the residents of Pripyat away. The residents thought they would be returning. They thought they were being evacuated for only three days. Pictures were left on walls. Sheets were left on beds. Food was left in refrigerators. Dishes were left in cupboards. Clothes were left in closets. Schoolbooks were left in desks. Stores were left filled with goods.

Pripyat was built in the 1970s. It was called the "City of the Future." All of its residents, including 15,400 children, were evacuated on April 27, 1986. No one knew they would never return. No one knew that the city was being abandoned forever. Pripyat was abandoned because of a terrible accident. The accident was at Chernobyl. Chernobyl was a nuclear power plant. A nuclear reactor had exploded.

Energy for a nuclear reactor comes from fission. Fission is the splitting of an atomic nucleus. A nucleus is the center of an atom. When the nucleus of an element such as uranium is split, large amounts of energy are released. When the reactor exploded at Chernobyl, tremendous amounts of radioactive particles were released into the atmosphere. When something is radioactive, it releases energy as it breaks down, or decays, into a form with a more stable nucleus. This process and energy is called radiation. Radiation in high amounts is deadly.

Pripyat was abandoned because of its level of radiation. Its level was deathly high. 76 surrounding villages were abandoned, too. Pripyat will be unsafe for a long time. It will be unsafe for at least 600 years. That is how long it will take for the present radioactive particles to decay to a safe level.

The Abandoned City of the Future

Quiz

After reading the story, answer the questions.
Fill in the circle next to the correct answer.

1. This story is mainly about
   a. what happened to a town.
   b. high levels of radiation.
   c. what the residents of Pripyat were like.
   d. how an accident happened at a nuclear power plant.

2. Which sentence from the story is the least important?
   a. "A nuclear reactor had exploded."
   b. "Radiation in high amounts is deadly."
   c. "No one knew the city was being abandoned forever."
   d. "Ukraine is known for its flat, fertile plains called steppes."

3. About how old was the city of Pripyat before it was abandoned?
   a. 3 days
   b. 15 years
   c. 25 years
   d. 600 years

4. People were most likely told that they were being evacuated for a short time only so that they would
   a. find a seat on one of the 2,000 buses.
   b. not sell what they were leaving behind.
   c. leave more quickly and not take too much.
   d. be in areas with higher levels of radiation.

5. Think about how the word *release* relates to *trap*. Which words relate in the same way?

   release : trap

   a. decay : rot
   b. evacuate : stay
   c. explode : burst
   d. abandon : leave

New Words

Ant Farmers

**These are new words to practice.
Say each word 10 times.**

- livestock
- aphids
- saliva
- consume
- antennae
- symbiosis
- mutualism
- beneficial

Before or after reading the story, write one sentence that contains at least one new word.

_____
_____
_____
_____

Story

Ant Farmers

Animals kept or raised on farms are called livestock. Some livestock farmers raise cattle. Others raise horses, sheep, or pigs. There is one kind of livestock farmer that does not raise any of these animals. Instead, this farmer raises aphids. Aphids are tiny insects. Aphids can cause great harm and destroy a farmer's plant crops by sucking a plant's juices from its leaves, stems, and roots. Aphids can also poison a plant with its saliva. When injected, an aphid's saliva can cause a plant leaf to curl up or even drop off. What kind of livestock farmer would raise aphids?

aphid

Aphid farmers are not human. Aphid farmers are a species, or particular kind, of ant. This particular ant species takes care of its aphid herds the same way human farmers take care of their livestock. Human farmers provide shelter for their herd. Ant farmers build mud shelters for aphids next to plant roots in their underground tunnels. Human farmers provide their animals with the kinds of foods they prefer to consume, or eat. Different aphids eat different kinds of plants, and ant farmers take their aphid herds outside to the specific plants they consume.

Human farmers protect their animals from predators. Ant farmers stand guard, ready to bite any predator that threatens their aphid herd. Aphids are sheltered and protected by ant farmers. What do the ants get from the aphids?

The ants get a constant supply of a sweet, nourishing liquid called honeydew. When an ant wants to eat, it simply strokes an aphid from behind with its antennae. The motion of the ant's antennae causes the aphid to release drops of nourishing honeydew that are quickly consumed by the ant.

The ant and the aphid are an example of what scientists call symbiosis. Symbiosis is when two different organisms have an unusual partnership. The symbiotic relationship between the ant and the aphid is one of mutualism. Mutualism is a beneficial relationship for both partners. When something is beneficial, it is helpful. Both the ant and the aphid are benefited, or helped, by their partnership.

Ant Farmers

Quiz

**After reading the story, answer the questions.
Fill in the circle next to the correct answer.**

1. This story is mainly about
   - ⓐ a symbiotic relationship.
   - ⓑ what aphids can do to plants.
   - ⓒ livestock farmers and their herds.
   - ⓓ how some ants get nourishing food.

2. A human livestock farmer would most likely raise
   - ⓐ corn.
   - ⓑ wheat.
   - ⓒ chickens.
   - ⓓ tomatoes.

3. Think about how the word *quickly* relates to *slowly*. Which words relate in the same way?

   | **quickly : slowly** |

   - ⓐ unusual : strange
   - ⓑ nourishing : healthy
   - ⓒ beneficial : harmful
   - ⓓ sheltered : protected

4. What does the ant get out of its symbiotic relationship with the aphid?
   - ⓐ food
   - ⓑ saliva
   - ⓒ shelter
   - ⓓ protection

5. Which relationship below is an example of mutualism?
   - ⓐ a lion chasing a herd of zebras
   - ⓑ a bird picking insects off of a giraffe's back
   - ⓒ a snake eating crocodile eggs before they hatch
   - ⓓ a fish jumping out of the water to catch a mosquito

©Teacher Created Resources, Inc.

The Human Ecosystem

**These are new words to practice.
Say each word 10 times.**

- ecosystem
- food chain
- food web
- consumed
- omnivores
- herbivores
- carnivores
- nutrients

Before or after reading the story, write one sentence that contains at least one new word.

_____
_____
_____
_____

The Human Ecosystem

An ecosystem is a certain area. It includes all the plants and animals in the area. It includes the non-living natural things, too, like rocks and soil. Among others, there are stream, forest, desert, and ocean ecosystems. Animals and plants within each ecosystem form food chains. A food chain is a pattern of eating and being eaten. For example, a plant is eaten by an insect, which is then eaten by a bird.

A food web is a network of connected food chains. The network forms when a member of one food chain eats a member of another food chain. For example, insects may be consumed, or eaten, by both birds and bears. When one thinks of a human's place in a food web, one often thinks of humans only as the consumer. After all, humans are omnivores. Omnivores are both herbivores and carnivores. Herbivores consume plants. Carnivores consume animals.

The truth is that humans are more than consumers. Each human is his or her own ecosystem! There are about 100 trillion cells inside a human. Most of these 100 trillion cells are not human! About only 10 trillion are human. The other 90 trillion cells are bacteria, fungi, and other microbes. All these cells are part of food chains. They are part of food webs. Many of these nonhuman cells are necessary for a healthy human ecosystem.

Take, for example, the bacteria in our gut and on our skin. There are at least 500 different species of bacteria that live inside the human gut. Their weight adds up to about 3.3 pounds (1.5 kg). Some bacteria break down carbohydrates. They make essential nutrients like vitamins K and B12. They are necessary.

There are about 1 trillion bacteria living on our skin. Some bacteria are the cause of body odor, but most of the bacteria are good for us. They are essential to healthy skin. The good bacteria keep the human ecosystem balanced. They keep nutrients from being eaten by harmful bacteria. If the bacteria were killed, the balance of the human ecosystem would change. Harmful bacteria might outnumber the good.

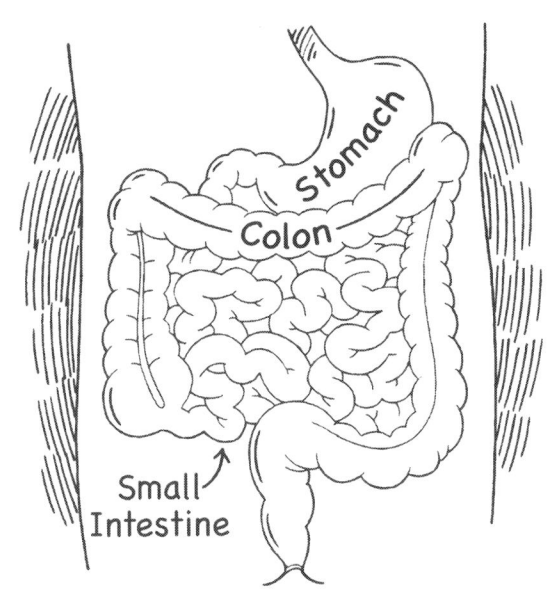

human digestive system

The Human Ecosystem

Quiz

After reading the story, answer the questions.
Fill in the circle next to the correct answer.

1. Which animal listed below is an herbivore?
   - ⓐ deer
   - ⓑ hawk
   - ⓒ bear
   - ⓓ snake

2. This story is mainly about
   - ⓐ consumers.
   - ⓑ nonhuman cells.
   - ⓒ the human ecosystem.
   - ⓓ connected food webs.

3. A plant is eaten by a fish, which is eaten by a dolphin. The plant, fish, and dolphin make up a
   - ⓐ food web.
   - ⓑ nutrient.
   - ⓒ ecosystem.
   - ⓓ food chain.

4. Think about how the word *consume* relates to *eat*. Which words relate in the same way?

   consume : eat

   - ⓐ harm : hurt
   - ⓑ work : play
   - ⓒ break : connect
   - ⓓ add : outnumber

5. From the story, one can tell that
   - ⓐ no bacteria are essential to human health.
   - ⓑ all bacteria are essential to human health.
   - ⓒ some bacteria are essential to human health.
   - ⓓ 500 bacteria species are essential to human health.

The Richter Scale

**These are new words to practice.
Say each word 10 times.**

- massive
- destruction
- seismologist
- seismograph
- trembling
- peaks
- inconvenient
- logarithms

Before or after reading the story, write one sentence that contains at least one new word.

_____

_____

_____

_____

The Richter Scale

There are millions of earthquakes around the world each year. Most are too weak to feel. Some earthquakes are quite powerful. They release massive amounts of energy. They cause much destruction. In fact, earthquakes cause more damage than any other kind of natural disaster.

Seismologists are scientists who study earthquakes. Seismologists use a special scale to measure the size of an earthquake. Charles F. Richter developed the scale in the 1930s. The scale is called the Richter scale. A seismograph is an instrument used to detect and measure earthquakes. A seismograph is a heavy weight hanging from a spring or wire. The weight appears to move, but it does not. It remains still as the earth waves up and down, trembling from an earthquake.

As the earth trembles, a pen attached to the seismograph records the earth's up and down movements. To develop his scale, Richter measured the peaks and valleys recorded by the seismograph. The largest earthquakes produced the highest peaks and lowest valleys. Smaller earthquakes produced smaller peaks and shallower valleys. Some earthquakes are millions of times more powerful than smaller ones. Richter knew using numbers in the millions would be inconvenient. Not wanting an inconvenient scale, Richter used a special form of mathematics known as logarithms.

seismograph

Richter's scale only used the numbers 1 to 10. Using logarithms, peak scale numbers increase by a factor of 10. For example, peaks that measure 2 are 10 times higher than those that measure 1. Peaks that measure 3 are 10 times higher than those that measure 2. They are 100 times higher than peaks that measure 1. Peaks that measure 10 are 10 times higher than those that measure 9. They are 1,000,000,000 times higher than peaks that measure 1.

An earthquake that measures less than 2.0 is not felt. One can feel indoor items shaking when an earthquake measures 4.0 to 4.9. An earthquake that measures 7.0 to 7.9 can cause serious damage over large areas. One measuring 9.0 or above can cause massive destruction over thousands of miles.

The Richter Scale

Quiz

After reading the story, answer the questions.
Fill in the circle next to the correct answer.

1. This story is mainly about

   a) earthquakes.
   b) an earthquake scale.
   c) numbers on a seismograph.
   d) a seismologist named Charles R. Richter.

2. On Richter's scale, a peak measuring 5 is

   a) 10 times higher than a peak measuring 4
   b) 10 times higher than a peak measuring 6
   c) 10 times higher than a peak measuring 8
   d) 10 times higher than a peak measuring 10

3. The only items damaged in an earthquake were some dishes. It is most likely that the earthquake measured

   a) 1.5
   b) 2.5
   c) 3.5
   d) 4.5

4. Which statement is not true?

   a) Richter invented the seismograph.
   b) A seismograph's weight does not move.
   c) Seismographs can detect earthquakes that cannot be felt.
   d) A seismograph records the earth's up and down movements.

5. Think about how the word *massive* relates to *enormous*. Which words relate in the same way?

   massive : enormous

   a) high : low
   b) shallow : deep
   c) special : common
   d) inconvenient : difficult

New Words

What the Meteorologists Found

**These are new words to practice.
Say each word 10 times.**

- meteorologists
- data
- observatory
- peak
- trends
- visibility
- precipitation
- aerosols

Before or after reading the story, write one sentence that contains at least one new word.

_____
_____
_____
_____

What the Meteorologists Found

Meteorology is a science. It is the science that studies weather, climate, and Earth's atmosphere. Meteorologists took data, or facts and figures. The data were taken from a meteorological observatory. The observatory was at the peak, or top, of a high mountain in China. The data had been collected from the high peak for the last 50 years.

Meteorologists looked at the data for trends. A trend is a general direction or course. The meteorologists found two interesting trends. They found that visibility had decreased. Visibility is the distance within which things can be seen. Before, one could see about 18.6 miles (30 km) from the peak. Over the years, visibility had decreased to about 6.2 miles (10 km).

The meteorologists found that precipitation had decreased. Precipitation is water in any form that falls from the sky. It is rain or snow. It is hail or sleet. Rainfall was less. It had dropped by as much as 17 percent when compared to neighboring areas. Visibility was less. Rainfall was less. What could explain the trends?

Meteorologists linked the trends to pollution. The pollution came from the air. It came from tiny particles, or aerosols. The aerosols were released into the air when fuel was burned. As more fuel was burned, more aerosols were released into the air. The number of aerosols built up. As the aerosols built up, visibility decreased. In addition, fewer raindrops formed. This is because raindrops form when water droplets in the air collide with each other. As aerosols in the air increase, fewer droplets collide with one another!

Meteorologists found that the decrease in highland precipitation was a trend observed in other places, too. It was observed in other countries. It was observed on other continents. This worldwide trend has a worldwide effect. Less precipitation in high mountain areas means less water in mountain streams. Less water in mountain streams means less water for people living downstream. It means less water for crops and people.

What the Meteorologists Found

Quiz

After reading the story, answer the questions.
Fill in the circle next to the correct answer.

1. This story is mainly about
   - (a) meteorology.
   - (b) some meteorological trends.
   - (c) data from a meteorological observatory.
   - (d) the decrease in highland precipitation.

2. From the story, one can tell that one way to stop the decrease of precipitation in highland areas is to
   - (a) decrease the number of aerosols released into the air.
   - (b) increase the number of aerosols released into the air.
   - (c) decrease the amount of water used from mountain streams.
   - (d) increase the amount of water used from mountain streams.

3. Think about how the word *rain* relates to *precipitation*. Which words relate in the same way?

   | rain : precipitation |

   - (a) gas : fuel
   - (b) gas : burn
   - (c) gas : aerosol
   - (d) gas : visibility

4. Visibility had decreased from the mountain peak by about
   - (a) 10.0 miles (16 km)
   - (b) 12.4 miles (20 km)
   - (c) 17.0 miles (27 km)
   - (d) 18.6 miles (30 km)

5. Which is most likely a trend?
   - (a) the color of people's eyes
   - (b) the number of teeth people have
   - (c) the length that people wear their hair
   - (d) the height people must be to ride a roller coaster

Observing the Jackal

New Words

These are new words to practice.
Say each word 10 times.

- agile
- ecologist
- organisms
- environment
- affected
- coexisted
- predator
- regurgitate

Before or after reading the story, write one sentence that contains at least one new word.

_____
_____
_____
_____

Observing the Jackal

Patricia Moehlman observed a jackal chasing a hyena away from its den. The hyena was huge compared to the jackal. The jackal weighed a mere 15 pounds (6.8 kg). The hyena weighed 120 pounds (54 kg). The jackal was agile, moving with quickness and ease. It darted up behind the hyena and bit it on its rear. Then, the agile jackal darted away before the clumsy hyena could even turn around.

Moehlman was a behavioral ecologist. Ecology is a branch of science. It is a field concerned with organisms and their relationships to the environment. Ecologists study how organisms and the environment are tied together. Moehlman studied animal behavior. She studied how an animal's behavior is affected, or changed, by its environment. Over the years, she observed many different kinds of animals.

Moehlman studied ground squirrels and kangaroo rats on an island off of the coast of Texas. Moehlman studied how the squirrels and rats coexisted, or lived together, in the same dune habitat. She studied chimpanzees in Tanzania. She studied wild burros in Death Valley, California. Now, on the Serengeti Plain in Tanzania, she was observing jackals. She observed how they coexisted with other animals. She studied how the environment affected their behavior.

jackal

Moehlman found that jackals go to great lengths to take care of their young pups. Mother jackals will move their pups to different dens about every two weeks. This helps keep the pups from being found by predators. If a predator finds the den, the jackal will chase it away. The jackal will chase much larger animals than itself. The jackal's agility helps it to protect its pups from larger, clumsier animals.

Jackals carry food to their dens for nursing mothers and pups. How is the food carried? It is carried in the jackal's stomach. At the den, the food is regurgitated. It is brought back up. Moehlman found that swallowing and regurgitating food fit the jackal's environment. If the jackal carried food in its mouth, larger predators could steal it. When the food was swallowed, it was kept safe. Predators could not steal it.

Quiz

Observing the Jackal

**After reading the story, answer the questions.
Fill in the circle next to the correct answer.**

1. What animal is not listed as being studied by Moehlman?

   ⓐ kangaroos
   ⓑ wild burros
   ⓒ chimpanzees
   ⓓ ground squirrels

2. This story is mainly about

   ⓐ how jackals carry food.
   ⓑ jackals and an observer.
   ⓒ what behavioral ecology is.
   ⓓ where Moehlman studied animals.

3. A behavioral ecologist would be least likely to be interested in studying

   ⓐ how air pollution can be lowered.
   ⓑ how a new road may block animal movement.
   ⓒ how birds build nests in places with few trees.
   ⓓ how polar bears may be affected by a warmer ocean.

4. Think about how the word *jackal* relates to *pup*. Which words relate in the same way?

   | jackal : pup |

   ⓐ calf : cow
   ⓑ lamb : sheep
   ⓒ foal : horse
   ⓓ cat : kitten

5. Which activity would most likely require the most agility?

   ⓐ listening to music
   ⓑ watching television
   ⓒ climbing a rope ladder
   ⓓ reading a book with 226 pages

©Teacher Created Resources, Inc.   #8037 Nonfiction Reading: Science

Disease Detectives

These are new words to practice.
Say each word 10 times.

- symptoms
- notified
- disease
- epidemiologist
- investigate
- source
- exhibiting
- toxins

Before or after reading the story, write one sentence that contains at least one new word.

_____

_____

_____

_____

Story

Disease Detectives

A group of people in Hawaii had gotten sick. All the people had the same symptoms, or signs, of the same illness. The Center for Disease Control (CDC) was notified, or informed. The CDC is a government organization. It was founded in 1946. Its mission is to examine and fight disease throughout the world. When the CDC was notified, it sent epidemiologists to investigate.

An epidemiologist is a "disease detective." Epidemiologists track diseases. They investigate disease outbreaks. First, they try to find out a disease's source, or where it came from. Then they try and find ways to stop the disease from spreading. The epidemiologists from the CDC questioned the people in Hawaii exhibiting, or showing, the same symptoms.

The epidemiologists found that everyone had attended the same picnic. They had eaten the same dish. The dish was made with boiled seaweed. Further questions showed that people who attended the picnic and did not exhibit symptoms had not eaten the dish. The epidemiologists had tracked the disease outbreak to the dish, but the investigation was far from over.

The seaweed dish was a traditional Hawaiian dish. It had been made and eaten for years and years. Why was it making people ill now? To find out, the epidemiologists took the dish remains. They tested the leftovers. They found toxins, or poisons, in the seaweed. The epidemiologists had found the disease-producing toxins, but their investigation was not over. The epidemiologists began on the next step. They asked more questions. They found out where the seaweed had been harvested.

Hawaii

The epidemiologists went to the site where the seaweed had been harvested. They swam around, looking for the toxin source. Finally, they found it. The source was found in a clump of seaweed. The source was a blue-green algae that was poisoning the seaweed. Epidemiologists had tracked the disease to its source. Now they could stop the outbreak. They could stop people from harvesting seaweed at that site. They could stop people from harvesting seaweed near blue-green algae.

Disease Detectives

Quiz

After reading the story, answer the questions.
Fill in the circle next to the correct answer.

1. This story is mainly about
   - a) investigating a disease outbreak.
   - b) the questions epidemiologists ask.
   - c) a traditional seaweed dish from Hawaii.
   - d) the Center for Disease Control's mission.

2. The toxin source was
   - a) the picnic.
   - b) the seaweed.
   - c) the blue-green algae.
   - d) the traditional seaweed dish.

3. Henry exhibited symptoms of being bored. Henry was most likely
   - a) eating.
   - b) reading.
   - c) yawning.
   - d) playing.

4. If many people were falling ill in a certain section of the city, epidemiologists might ask if the people
   - a) knew how to ride bicycles.
   - b) spoke more than one language.
   - c) were left handed or right handed.
   - d) had the same drinking-water source.

5. Think about how the word *founded* relates to *end*. Which words relate in the same way?

   | founded : end |

   - a) tracked : follow
   - b) exhibited : hide
   - c) notified : inform
   - d) harvested : gather

#8037 Nonfiction Reading: Science 128 ©Teacher Created Resources, Inc.

The Astronomer with the Metal Nose

These are new words to practice.
Say each word 10 times.

- partial
- solar
- eclipse
- awe

- astronomy
- celestial
- observatory
- supernova

Before or after reading the story, write one sentence that contains at least one new word.

_____
_____
_____
_____

The Astronomer with the Metal Nose

Tycho Brahe was 13 years old when he witnessed a partial solar eclipse. A solar eclipse occurs when the sun is blocked or hidden by the moon when it passes between the sun and Earth. During a partial solar eclipse, only part of the sun is blocked. The event filled Brahe with awe, or wonder. Brahe was awestruck that astronomers had predicted the event. The year was 1560.

Brahe decided to study astronomy. Astronomy is a science that studies the size, motion, and make-up of celestial bodies. Planets, moons, stars, and comets are all examples of celestial bodies. Brahe wanted to be an astronomer who could make accurate predictions. He wanted to be able to say what and when celestial events would take place.

Brahe was Danish. He was a brilliant man and a skilled astronomer. He built his own observatory. He filled it with specialized equipment. Brahe had developed the equipment for observing stars. The observatory was on a small island given to Brahe by the king of Denmark. Brahe's years of careful observations, at a time before the invention of the telescope, provided astronomers with accurate data. It helped younger astronomers like Johannes Kepler develop groundbreaking laws of planetary motion.

Tycho Brahe

Brahe observed a new star, or nova, in 1572. It was the first new star recorded in Europe since 125 B.C. During Brahe's time, astronomers still believed stars were fixed and could not change. We now know that Brahe observed a supernova. A supernova is the explosive death of a star. Brahe's observation of a supernova was evidence that stars were not fixed. They could change.

Brahe is known for his accurate observations, but he is also known for his nose. When Brahe was 18, he got in an argument with a fellow student. The argument was over a minor math problem. The argument grew so heated that the two students decided to have a duel. Brahe was injured in the duel, and part of his nose was sliced off. Brahe had a metal replacement made. The replacement was made of gold and silver.

Brahe's equipment

The Astronomer with the Metal Nose

Quiz

**After reading the story, answer the questions.
Fill in the circle next to the correct answer.**

1. How old was Brahe when he lost part of his nose?

   a) 13
   b) 15
   c) 18
   d) 21

2. This story is mainly about

   a) Brahe's nose.
   b) an astronomer.
   c) observations on celestial bodies.
   d) what astronomer's believed long ago.

3. If a person is overshadowed or outdone by another one's act, one could say that the person has been

   a) partial.
   b) observed.
   c) eclipsed.
   d) predicted.

4. Think about how the word *Denmark* relates to *Danish*. Which words relate in the same way?

   Denmark : Danish

   a) China : Asian
   b) France : French
   c) Germany : European
   d) Texas : United States

5. From the story, one can tell that

   a) Brahe did not use a telescope.
   b) Brahe was unhappy with his metal nose.
   c) Brahe was not good at solving math problems.
   d) Brahe did not care about celestial predictions.

Taking a Volcano's Pulse

These are new words to practice.
Say each word 10 times.

- pulse
- monitor
- predicted
- seismometer

- magma
- concentration
- bulge
- obvious

Before or after reading the story, write one sentence that contains at least one new word.

_____
_____
_____
_____

Taking a Volcano's Pulse

A pulse is any regular beat. Doctors take patient's pulses. Taking a pulse helps a doctor monitor, or keep an eye on, his or her patient's health. Scientists who study volcanoes take a volcano's pulse. It helps them monitor what is happening inside the volcano. Why does a scientist monitor a volcano's pulse? How is it done?

Lives can be saved when a volcanic eruption can be predicted, or foretold. If a volcano eruption is predicted, warnings can be issued. People can be evacuated. Roadblocks can be set up. It is impossible to know exactly when a volcano might erupt, but scientists have learned to base their predictions on a volcano's pulse, or elements of its behavior.

Scientists look for certain earthquake patterns. They use seismometers. They plant seismometers around the volcano to determine the size and location of earthquakes. The seismometers help scientists track the subsurface movement of magma. Magma is molten, or melted, rock. This is because magma that is pushed up to the surface puts pressure on surrounding, cooler rocks. The pressure causes the rocks to crack and the earth to shake.

Scientists check for gases and heat being released by the volcano. They use a special device to measure the concentration of different gases. This is because as magma rises, gases bubble out. Scientists look for high concentrations of gases they know are released before an eruption. Scientists use weather satellites to check for heat being released by the rising magma. They also look for increased steam, as the magma can boil surrounding groundwater.

Scientists check for changes in the volcano's shape. They look for parts that bulge, or swell. They use special devices that measure big, obvious bulges and small, less obvious bulges. The bulges are formed as rising magma pushes out sections of rocks. Sometimes scientists put themselves in danger as they take a volcano's pulse. This is because they may be planting devices or collecting gas samples when the volcano starts to erupt.

Taking a Volcano's Pulse

Quiz

After reading the story, answer the questions.
Fill in the circle next to the correct answer.

1. This story is mainly about
   - (a) volcanoes around the world.
   - (b) scientists who study volcanoes.
   - (c) when volcano eruption warnings are given.
   - (d) what is checked when volcanoes are monitored.

2. Why do scientists plant seismometers?
   - (a) to measure big and small bulges.
   - (b) to test for heat released by rising magma.
   - (c) to track the subsurface movement of magma.
   - (d) to check the concentration of gases being released.

3. Think about how the word *monitor* relates to *ignore*. Which words relate in the same way?

   monitor : ignore

   - (a) quake : shake
   - (b) release : trap
   - (c) track : follow
   - (d) predict : foretell

4. Which paragraph answers the question, "Why does a scientists monitor a volcano's pulse?"
   - (a) paragraph 1
   - (b) paragraph 2
   - (c) paragraph 3
   - (d) paragraph 5

5. Fill a balloon with air. Squeeze it in the middle. It will _____ out on both sides.
   - (a) bulge
   - (b) pulse
   - (c) erupt
   - (d) concentrate

#8037 Nonfiction Reading: Science ©Teacher Created Resources, Inc.

New Words

The King of Soaring

**These are new words to practice.
Say each word 10 times.**

- albatross
- soaring
- avian
- effortlessly
- exceptionally
- wingspan
- extended
- prevailing

Before or after reading the story, write one sentence that contains at least one new word.

_____
_____
_____
_____

Story

The King of Soaring

An albatross is the king of soaring. This avian wonder can glide effortlessly over the open ocean for months at a time. It can reach speeds over 70 miles (112.6 km) per hour. It can stay aloft almost continuously, even sleeping on the wing! An albatross may fly millions of miles in its lifetime. It may circle the globe, time after time. Yet this bird rarely has to flap its wings! How is this possible?

Albatrosses have exceptionally long wings. Their wings are very narrow compared to their length. The largest albatross species, the wandering albatross, can have a wingspan measuring 11.5 feet (3.5 m)! Despite this exceptionally long wingspan, the albatross's wings measure only 6 to 9 inches (15 to 23 cm) across! No other avian species has this large of a contrast between its wingspan and its wing width.

The albatross's wing shape is what allows the bird to soar effortlessly over the water without flapping its winds. When albatrosses fly, their wings are extended, like those of a glider. They ride the wind, soaring on air currents.

albatross

Air close to the surface of the water moves slower than the air at upper levels. When an albatross dives toward the water with wings extended, its body meets less air resistance. It gains speed.

Close to the water surface, the albatross suddenly turns. It uses the speed it gained going down to carry itself up. It rises up higher and higher as its wings catch stronger and stronger layers of wind. The albatross travels thousands of miles, swooping up and down as if on a roller coaster, using the energy of the wind to keep moving.

An albatross's dependence on wind energy explains why this avian species is not often found close to the equator. Prevailing winds are winds that blow most of the time. There are few prevailing winds close to the equator. Albatrosses are found north and south of the equator where there are bands of prevailing winds.

The King of Soaring

**After reading the story, answer the questions.
Fill in the circle next to the correct answer.**

1. This story is mainly about
   - ⓐ an avian wonder.
   - ⓑ using wind energy.
   - ⓒ the king of birds.
   - ⓓ an albatross's wings.

2. Which pair of adjectives best describes an albatross in flight?
   - ⓐ rising and flapping
   - ⓑ soaring and stopping
   - ⓒ gliding and swimming
   - ⓓ dipping and wheeling

3. For its wingspan, an albatross has an exceptionally
   - ⓐ wide wing width
   - ⓑ large wing width
   - ⓒ narrow wing width
   - ⓓ extended wing width

4. Most likely an albatross mainly eats
   - ⓐ animals that fly.
   - ⓑ animals that live on land.
   - ⓒ animals that live deep in the water.
   - ⓓ animals that live near the water surface.

5. Think about how the word *avian* relates to *bird*. Which words relate in the same way?

   | **avian : bird** |

   - ⓐ meow : cat
   - ⓑ horse : foal
   - ⓒ canine : dog
   - ⓓ jump : kangaroo

New Words

Tuberculosis and a Cave

These are new words to practice.
Say each word 10 times.

- tuberculosis
- insidious
- contracted
- persistent
- mammoth
- surveyed
- humidity
- antibiotics

Before or after reading the story, write one sentence that contains at least one new word.

_____

_____

_____

_____

Tuberculosis and a Cave

Tuberculosis, or TB, is a disease. For many years, no one knew much about the disease. Doctors knew that the disease was worldwide. They knew that the disease's onset was insidious, or more dangerous than it seems to be. Tuberculosis was an insidious disease because doctors had no cure for it. Doctors did not even know how a person contracted, or came to have, TB.

Doctors did know that when a patient contracted TB, the patient lost his or her energy. The patient lost weight and developed a persistent cough. When something is persistent, it lasts for some time. It goes on and on. Over time, the cough would get worse. The patient would begin to cough up blood, then die.

Mammoth Cave's name fits, because the cave is mammoth, or very large. Located in Kentucky, Mammoth Cave is one of the largest cave systems in the world. Over 350 miles (560 km) of passageways have been surveyed, or mapped. Passageways have been found at depths of 450 feet (137 m) below the surface. Huge underground chambers, or rooms, and pits so deep they appear bottomless have been surveyed, as well as rivers containing eyeless cavefish.

There is a link between Mammoth Cave and TB. The tie is historical. John Croghan was a doctor who bought Mammoth Cave in 1839. Croghan, like other doctors of his time, did not know how one contracted TB or how it was spread. Croghan built a TB hospital deep in Mammoth Cave. He hoped that the constant temperature and humidity would lead to his dying patients' recovery. The temperature of Mammoth Cave is a cool 54°F (12.2°C). The humidity, or amount of moisture in the air, is very low.

Although desperate enough to move to constant darkness deep underground, Croghan's patients were not helped. Croghan was forced to close his hospital, and Croghan himself contracted and died of TB. Today we know that TB is caused by a tubercle bacillus, or type of bacteria. Doctors treat TB patients with antibiotics. Antibiotics are medicines designed to kill bacteria.

Tuberculosis and a Cave

Quiz

**After reading the story, answer the questions.
Fill in the circle next to the correct answer.**

1. This story is mainly about
   - (a) a cave and a disease.
   - (b) tuberculosis treatment.
   - (c) a doctor and a hospital.
   - (d) Mammoth Cave in Kentucky.

2. Mammoth Cave's low humidity meant that the air inside the cave was very
   - (a) dry.
   - (b) hot.
   - (c) cold.
   - (d) moist.

3. Croghan's patients were willing to move away from their families to the inner blackness of an underground cave. Most likely, Croghan's patients
   - (a) wanted to explore and survey passages.
   - (b) felt they could be helped with antibiotics.
   - (c) thought the constant darkness would cure them.
   - (d) believed it was their only chance at recovery.

4. This story does not answer which question?
   - (a) What causes tuberculosis?
   - (b) How was Mammoth Cave formed?
   - (c) Where is Mammoth Cave located?
   - (d) When did Dr. Croghan buy Mammoth Cave?

5. Think about how the word *mammoth* relates to *small*. Which words relate in the same way?

   | mammoth : small |

   - (a) blind : sightless
   - (b) surveyed : mapped
   - (c) temperature : cold
   - (d) persistent : temporary

Answer Sheets

Student Name: _____

Title of Reading Passage: _____
_____

1. (a) (b) (c) (d)
2. (a) (b) (c) (d)
3. (a) (b) (c) (d)
4. (a) (b) (c) (d)
5. (a) (b) (c) (d)

Student Name: _____

Title of Reading Passage: _____
_____

1. (a) (b) (c) (d)
2. (a) (b) (c) (d)
3. (a) (b) (c) (d)
4. (a) (b) (c) (d)
5. (a) (b) (c) (d)

Bibliography

Associated Press. "Japanese Man Recites Pi From Memory to 100,000 Decimal Places, Claims World Record." *International Herald Tribune.* 4 October 2006.

Bankston, John. *Joseph Lister and the Story of Antiseptics.* Mitchell Lane Publishers, Inc., 2005.

"Beaumont, William." *The New Encyclopedia Britannica*, volume 2, page 23. Encyclopedia Britannica, Inc., 1990.

Biello, David. "Drought-Making Pollutants." *Scientific American.* May 2007: 37.

Blassingame, Wyatt. *The Strange Armadillo.* Dodd, Mead, & Company, 1983.

"Botulism," *The New Encyclopedia Britannica*, volume 2, page 415–416. Encyclopedia Britannica, Inc., 1990.

De Leo, Maryann. "Chernobyl Revisited." *Discover.* June 2007: 68–75.

Dumiak, Michael. "Lifting the Winter Dark." *Scientific American.* April 2006: 20–22.

Editors, *Secrets of the Universe.* "Animals in Space." *Secrets of the Universe*, Mission Log, Card 8. International Masters Publishers AB.

———. "Tycho Brahe." *Secrets of the Universe*, Space Pioneers, Card 11. International Masters Publishers, AB.

Ellis, Richard. *Singing Whales and Flying Squid: The Discovery of Marine Life.* The Lyons Press, The Globe Pequot Press, 2005.

Farndon, John. *Aluminum.* Benchmark Books, Marshall Cavendish, 2001.

Feldman, David. *What Are Hyenas Laughing At, Anyway?* G.P Putnam's Sons, 1995.

"50, 100 & 150 Years Ago From Scientific American: CSI Prussia." Scientific American. April 2006 : 16.

Foster, Ruth. *Take Five Minutes*: *Fascinating Facts About Geography.* Teacher Created Resources, Inc., 2003.

———. Take Five Minutes: *Fascinating Facts and Stories for Reading and Critical Thinking.* Teacher Created Resources, Inc., 2001.

Glausiusz, Josie. "The Beacon Bird of Climate Change." *Discover.* April 2007: 14.

———. "Your Body Is a Planet." *Discover.* June 2007: 44–45.

"Gold," *The New Encyclopedia Britannica*, volume 5, page 336–337. Encyclopedia Britannica, Inc., 1990.

Greenberg, Keith Elliot. *Disease Detective.* Birchbark Press, Inc., 1998.

Harman, Amanda. *Armadillos.* Grolier, Scholastic Library Publishing, 2004.

Holmes, Bonnie. *Quaking Aspen.* Carolrhoda Books, Inc., 1999.

Johnson, Sylvia A. *Albatrosses of Midway Island.* Carolrhoda Books, Inc., 1990.

Kahn, Jennifer. "The Extreme Sport of Origami." *Discover.* July 2006: 60–63.

Kruglinski, Susan. "Whatever Happened to Moon Rocks?" *Discover.* July 2006: 14.

Landau, Elaine. *Joined at Birth: The Lives of Conjoined Twins.* Franklin Watts, Grolier Publishing, 1997.

Lanting, Frans. *Animal Athletes: Olympians of the Wild World.* The Nature Company and Andrews and McMeel, 1996.

Lindop, Laurie. *Probing Volcanoes.* Twenty-First Century Books, The Millbrook Press, Inc., 2003.

Lockwood, Sophie. *Cobras.* The Child's World, 2006.

Bibliography

Mammoth Cave Glossary. Website: *http://www.nps.gov/maca/learnhome/glossary.htm*

Martin, James. *The Spitting Cobras of Africa*. Capstone Press, 1995.

Moss, Carol. *Science in Ancient Mesopotamia*. Franklin Watts, Grolier Publishing, 1998.

National Park Service. "Mammoth Cave" (Park Brochure). U.S. Department of the Interior, 2007.

Newton, David E. *Earthquakes*. Franklin Watts, 1993.

Pardellas, Juan Manuel. "Scientists Study Earth's Missing Crust." *The Associated Press*. 6 March 2007.

Patent, Dorothy Hinshaw. *Secrets of the Ice Man*. Benchmark Books, Marshall Cavendish, 1999.

Pringle, Laurence. *Jackal Woman: Exploring the World of Jackals*. Charles Scribner's Sons, MacMillan Publishing Company, 1993.

Ruvinsky, Jessica. "Meet the New Continent." *Discover*. October 2006: 15.

Schueller, Gretel H. "Escort Service." *Audubon*. January–February 2007: 17.

Scordato, Ellen (Editor). *The New York Public Library Desk Reference*, Fourth Edition. Hyperion, 2002.

Senker, Cath. *Rosalind Franklin*. Raintree Steck-Vaughn Publishers, 2003.

Shaw, Dan. "Warmer Weather's Here. Potholes and Road Work, Too." *Journal and Courier*. 14 March 2007: A1 and A8.

Silverstein, Alvin and Virginia, and Laura Silverstein Nunn. *Burns and Blisters*. Franklin Watts, Scholastic, Inc., 2002.

———. Plate Tectonics. Twenty-First Century Books, The Millbrook Press, Inc., 1998.

———. *Poisoning*. Franklin Watts, Scholastic, Inc., 2003.

———. *Symbiosis*. Twenty-First Century Books, The Millbrook Press, Inc., 1998.

Simpson, Ken, and Nicolas Day and Peter Trusler. *The Princeton Field Guide to the Birds of Australia*. Princeton University Press, 1996.

Spangenburg, Ray and Diane K. Moser. *The History of Science From the Ancient Greeks to the Scientific Revolution*. Facts on File, Inc. 1993.

Spilsbury, Louise and Richard. *Classification from Mammals to Fungi*. Heinemann Library, Reed Elsevier, Inc., 2004.

Swanson, Diane. *Burp!: The Most Interesting Book You'll Ever Read About Eating*. Kids Can Press, Ltd., 2001.

Tocci, Salvatore. *Aluminum*. Children's Press, Scholastic Inc., 2005.

"Tuberculosis." *The New Encyclopedia Britannica*, volume 12, page 24. Encyclopedia Britannica, Inc., 1990.

Twist, Clint. *Fleas*. Gareth Stevens Publishing, 2006.

Wade, Peter (Editor). *Every Australian Bird Illustrated*. Rigby Limited, 1975.

Zach, Kim K. *Hidden From History: The Lives of Eight American Women Scientists*. Avisson Press, Inc., 2002.

Answer Key

What Swallowed Camels
1. A 4. C
2. D 5. A
3. B

Why Mari Said, "No"!
1. D 4. A
2. B 5. D
3. C

The Amazing Jumper
1. D 4. A
2. A 5. C
3. B

Conjoined Twins
1. B 4. C
2. D 5. A
3. C

Identical Trees
1. D 4. B
2. C 5. B
3. D

The Extreme Sport of Paper Folding
1. B 4. C
2. D 5. C
3. B

What Was Not a Grave
1. A 4. A
2. B 5. D
3. C

A Town That Gets No Sun
1. C 4. B
2. C 5. A
3. B

45,000 Years of Penguin Droppings
1. C 4. A
2. B 5. B
3. A

Finding the Counterfeit Coin
1. C 4. A
2. B 5. C
3. D

Amphibian Escort
1. B 4. A
2. D 5. D
3. A

Blisters—To Pop or Not
1. B 4. A
2. C 5. A
3. C

The World's First Life Preserver
1. B 4. B
2. C 5. C
3. D

What Is It?
1. A 4. B
2. C 5. D
3. C

Getting Stung on Purpose
1. D 4. D
2. A 5. C
3. C

A Season for Potholes
1. A 4. B
2. D 5. A
3. B

The True Story Behind DNA
1. D 4. A
2. C 5. C
3. B

Strange Stomach Stories
1. B 4. C
2. D 5. D
3. B

A Parachute and a Shark
1. A 4. D
2. B 5. B
3. C

A True Case from 1856
1. C 4. D
2. B 5. B
3. D

What Came First
1. D 4. C
2. C 5. A
3. D

The Most Expensive Rattle
1. B 4. A
2. A 5. C
3. D

The Mammal with a Suit of Armor
1. D 4. B
2. C 5. C
3. A

Moon Rocks
1. C 4. A
2. A 5. B
3. B

Injecting Poison on Purpose
1. A 4. A
2. B 5. B
3. C

The 5,000-Year-Old Man
1. C 4. B
2. A 5. D
3. D

A Quiver of Cobras
1. B 4. D
2. C 5. B
3. A

The Price of a Crooked Finger
1. B 4. D
2. D 5. A
3. C

May I Draw a Round Perimeter?
1. C 4. A
2. D 5. D
3. B

Why Warm Flowers?
1. B 4. D
2. D 5. C
3. A

Space Animals
1. D 4. A
2. C 5. A
3. C

"Operation Successful, Patient Died"
1. D 4. A
2. A 5. B
3. D

The Missing Crust
1. D 4. D
2. B 5. C
3. A

The Abandoned City of the Future
1. A 4. C
2. D 5. B
3. B

Ant Farmers
1. A 4. A
2. C 5. B
3. C

The Human Ecosystem
1. A 4. A
2. C 5. C
3. D

The Richter Scale
1. B 4. A
2. A 5. D
3. D

What the Meteorologists Found
1. B 4. B
2. A 5. C
3. A

Observing the Jackal
1. D 4. D
2. B 5. C
3. A

Disease Detectives
1. A 4. D
2. C 5. B
3. C

The Astronomer with the Metal Nose
1. C 4. B
2. B 5. A
3. C

Taking a Volcano's Pulse
1. D 4. B
2. C 5. A
3. B

The King of Soaring
1. A 4. D
2. D 5. C
3. C

Tuberculosis and a Cave
1. A 4. B
2. A 5. B
3. D

Made in the USA
Lexington, KY
18 January 2018